S0-CGQ-607

SEP 19 '95

UNION ~~~~~~~OL DIST,
~~~~~~~~ AX HIGHWAY
GR~~~~~LEY, CA 95945

DISCARD

FAMOUS LIVES

The Story of
HILLARY RODHAM CLINTON
First Lady of the United States

By Joyce Milton

Gareth Stevens Publishing
MILWAUKEE

For a free color catalog describing Gareth Stevens' list of high-quality books, call 1-800-542-2595 (USA) or 1-800-461-9120 (Canada). Gareth Stevens' Fax: (414) 225-0377.

Library of Congress Cataloging-in-Publication Data

Milton, Joyce.
    The story of Hillary Rodham Clinton : First Lady of the United
States / by Joyce Milton.
      p. cm. — (Famous lives)
    Includes index.
    Summary: Examines the childhood, family life, and social and
political activities of this powerful and important First Lady.
    ISBN 0-8368-1381-2
    1. Clinton, Hillary Rodham—Juvenile literature. 2. Clinton,
Bill, 1946- —Juvenile literature. 3. Presidents' spouses—United
States—Biography—Juvenile literature. [1. Clinton, Hillary
Rodham. 2. First ladies. 3. Women—Biography.] I. Title.
II. Series: Famous lives (Milwaukee, Wis.)
E887.C55M55   1995
973.929'092—dc20
[B]   95-18325

The events described in this book are true. They have been carefully researched and
excerpted from authentic biographies, writings, and commentaries. No part of this
biography has been fictionalized. To learn more about Hillary Rodham Clinton, refer
to the list of books and videos at the back of this book or ask your librarian to recommend
other fine books and videos.

This edition first published in 1995 by
Gareth Stevens Publishing
1555 North RiverCenter Drive, Suite 201
Milwaukee, Wisconsin 53212, USA

Original © 1994 by Parachute Press, Inc. as a Yearling Biography.
Published by arrangement with Bantam Doubleday Dell Books for Young Readers,
a division of Bantam Doubleday Dell Publishing Group, Inc.
Additional end matter © 1995 by Gareth Stevens, Inc.

Cover photo: © White House/Sipa Press

All rights to this edition reserved to Gareth Stevens, Inc. No part of this book may be
reproduced, stored in a retrieval system, or transmitted in any form or by any means,
electronic, mechanical, photocopying, recording, or otherwise without the prior
written permission of the publisher except for the inclusion of brief quotations in
an acknowledged review.

Printed in the United States of America

1 2 3 4 5 6 7 8 9 99 98 97 96 95

Contents

Preface

When the United States of America was formed more than two hundred years ago, no one gave much thought to the president's wife. Our United States Constitution doesn't even mention the First Lady. It wasn't long, though, before Americans began looking to the president's wife as a role model. As our country grew, so did the duties of the First Lady.

Hillary Rodham Clinton has been one of the most important First Ladies in American history. She has changed our ideas about what a First Lady can be and do. Today many women have careers. But Hillary was the first career woman to be married to a United States president.

From the time she was a little girl, Hillary seemed destined for success. Her parents taught her to study hard and rely on her own strong sense of right and wrong. In school and college she was a leader. At a time when few young women thought about going to law school, Hillary did, and did it well. She was one of the top students in her law school class.

Family was always very important to Hillary. When she decided to marry Bill Clinton, she had to change her career plans and settle in a part of the country

1

where she knew very few people. As the wife of a political officeholder, she had to learn to live in the public eye.

When Bill Clinton was elected president, Hillary Rodham Clinton took on the job of finding ways to reform America's health-care system. She also had to run the White House and help her daughter, Chelsea, get used to being famous. Like many women today, Hillary was juggling several different roles—wife, mother, and professional woman. But as the president's wife, she faced a special challenge. The whole country was watching to see how well this new type of First Lady would succeed.

Growing Up in Park Ridge

The little blond girl held her bat ready. As the baseball sailed over the corner of home plate, she swung with all her might. The bat fanned the air.

Try as she would, she couldn't hit a curveball.

Out on the pitcher's mound her father shook his head.

"Okay, now, Hillary," he said. "Let's try again. This time keep your eyes on the ball."

Once more he made his windup and released the ball. Hillary swung. And this time her bat made contact. The ball sailed over the infield, a solid hit.

Hillary Diane Rodham loved baseball. It was her father's favorite sport, and she shared his enthusiasm. Hillary and her dad often went to major-league games together. By the time she was ten, Hillary knew the names of all the players on their home team, the Chicago Cubs. She also knew their averages, and she could confidently swap baseball statistics with the boys in her class.

Hillary liked to play softball and sometimes baseball. Her favorite position was second base. On Sundays after church she and her father would stop by the local Little League field, and he would help her work on her batting skills.

Hillary's parents, Dorothy and Hugh Rodham, spent a lot of time with their children. In many ways their family life was almost ideal. When Hillary was born on October 26, 1947, her parents lived in an apartment in Chicago. But when she was three years old, the Rodhams decided to move to the suburbs. They chose a yellow brick house on a quiet street in Park Ridge, west of the city. Hillary's brother Hugh was born a few months after the family moved. A second brother, Tony, came along four years later.

Park Ridge was a quiet town with tree-lined streets and green parks. It was a safe community, with very little crime. Most people didn't even bother to lock their doors at night. In that way Park Ridge was like thousands of other suburban towns across the country.

Park Ridge was a wealthier town than most. Some families lived in fancy homes surrounded by gardens. But the Rodham house was just roomy and comfortable. And their neighborhood was a friendly one. Many of the residents were young couples like Hugh and Dorothy. They had all begun having children when they were able to settle down after World War II. "There must have been forty or fifty children within a few blocks' radius of our house," Hillary's mother remembered.

Hillary and the other boys and girls played freely in the neighborhood streets. They ran through their neighbors' backyards and organized games of hide-

and-seek that covered whole blocks. The elementary school they attended was within walking distance. When classes let out, they would race home, jump on their bikes, and ride through the neighborhood. In the winter they went ice skating. Sometimes they would buy soda at a soda fountain called the Happy House. As long as they were home on time for dinner, their parents didn't worry about their playing outside on their own.

At Halloween everyone put on costumes and went trick or treating. With so many children and houses in the neighborhood, Halloween was bound to be a big event. A favorite stop was the house of a Miss Lessard, down the street from the Rodhams. Miss Lessard kept Pomeranian dogs as pets. She loved her dogs so much that when one of them died, she would have its body stuffed. She kept the stuffed dogs in a glass case in her living room.

But even in a friendly town like Park Ridge, there were bullies. When Hillary was four, she had a problem with another girl about her age. The girl was the leader of a group of kids in the neighborhood. For some reason she seemed to make a special point of tormenting Hillary. Maybe it was because she thought Hillary wouldn't fight back. A few times the girl even beat Hillary up, sending her home in tears.

Dorothy Rodham didn't approve of fighting. But she also believed that her children had to learn to stand up for themselves. Once when Hillary came home crying, her mother said, "The next time she hits you, I want you to hit back."

Hillary went back outside, where the bully was waiting for her. The bully started calling Hillary names, and then she started hitting. But this time Hillary didn't run home. She decided to try to defend herself, even though she didn't know anything about fighting. She just closed her eyes and swung back. To her surprise, the girl went down when Hillary struck her. That was the last time the bully ever picked on Hillary.

Dorothy Rodham was proud of her daughter's courage. "I never had to worry about Hillary," she said.

But Hillary's parents also taught their daughter to get along with others. The whole family loved card and board games and often played them together. Mr. Rodham taught all three of his children to play pinochle, his favorite card game. Although the children were competitive, Hillary and her brothers learned to play by the rules and to be good sports if they lost.

Hillary's father had taught physical education in the navy. He loved sports. Sometimes he even turned household chores into competitions. If the lawn needed weeding, Hillary and her brothers would try to see who could pull the most dandelions. They got a penny for each dandelion they picked.

Dorothy Rodham's hobby was reading. Even though she didn't graduate from college, she never lost her interest in learning. As her children got older and she had more free time, she signed up for Spanish and other college courses. She wasn't working for a degree, but only to improve her mind. Often she picked courses that had the longest and hardest reading lists.

Mrs. Rodham wanted all of her children to love school. When they were very young, she encouraged them to look forward to starting first grade. "Education is a great adventure," she would say. "Learn for the sake of learning."

Right from the start Hillary loved school. She was a leader both in class and in after-school activities. She became a Brownie and enjoyed going to meetings. When she was old enough to become a Girl Scout, she earned every single merit badge that was offered.

When Hillary was in sixth grade at the Eugene Field Elementary School, her class was assigned a teacher who was known to be very strict. Some of the kids were a bit scared of Mrs. King. Not Hillary! She got such good grades and was so confident in class that Mrs. King wanted to teach her again. Mrs. King transferred grades the next year so that she would have Hillary in her class again. "Hillary was Mrs. King's favorite human being on earth," one classmate said.

If anything, Hillary was almost too good. She was never late for school. And no one could remember her ever breaking the rules.

Hillary liked doing things with other children. But when some of her girlfriends decided to try piercing their ears, she wanted no part of the experiment. She wasn't the type to do something just to be part of the crowd. But her independence didn't keep her from having many friends. She laughed a lot and was very loyal.

As Hillary got older, her time was taken up with many different activities. In addition to attending Girl Scout meetings, she took ballet and piano lessons. Hillary succeeded at almost everything she tried—except piano lessons. She studied for a while with Miss Lessard, the woman who kept her stuffed pet dogs in the living room. She also took lessons from a man who was considered a very good teacher. Even so, Hillary had trouble learning the simplest pieces. She could pick out notes with her right hand. Or she could pick them out with her left hand. But she could never quite make her two hands play well together. Hillary was relieved when she was finally allowed to stop taking lessons.

Lessons in Life

Hillary had a comfortable, busy life in Park Ridge. But it hadn't always been that easy for her parents. Hugh and Dorothy Rodham grew up during the Great Depression of the 1930s. This was a time when many people were unemployed and didn't always have enough food to eat. Hugh and Dorothy's families were very poor during those years.

Hugh Rodham attended school in Scranton, Pennsylvania. His father worked in a factory that made lace. Some of Hugh's relatives worked in the coal mines. For a time Hugh also went to work as a miner to help his family and to earn money for school. Even so, he might not have been able to go to college if he hadn't been a good athlete. He won a football scholarship to Penn State University and majored in physical education.

When Hugh graduated, unemployment and poverty were still high. There were no jobs for young men with college degrees. Hugh got work at the lace factory, where he did hard jobs like loading heavy boxes. Playing football in college had made him strong.

In time Hugh moved to Chicago, where he became a salesman for a company that made curtains. One day a pretty young woman named Dorothy Howell came into the office to apply for a job as a secretary. Hugh saw her in the waiting room and stopped to talk. That was how Hillary's parents met. Dorothy had been born in Chicago, the daughter of a fireman. As a girl she lived in California, but after high school she returned to her hometown to work.

Hugh and Dorothy met in 1937, but at first they couldn't afford to get married. In 1942 the United States was involved in World War II. Hugh went into the navy, where he was a physical education instructor. Another five years went by before Hugh and Dorothy could start a family. When they became parents, Hugh and Dorothy Rodham wanted to give Hillary and her brothers the things they had never had. But both of them also worried that the children would be spoiled by having too much. This was especially true of Mr. Rodham. He wanted to make sure his children knew how hard life could be.

When the war ended, Hillary's father started his own curtain business. He made draperies for office buildings and other special customers. Mr. Rodham's curtain business was successful, but it was never a large company. There were only a few employees.

Sometimes a big order would come in, and Hillary's brothers would have to go in to work at the factory on weekends to help out. They never got paid, at least not in cash. "Maybe we got an extra baked potato at dinner," Tony Rodham said. "We were probably the only kids in the whole suburb who didn't get an allowance."

Hillary didn't have to work in the factory, but she

earned spending money by baby-sitting. After she started high school, Hillary got a certificate as a swimming teacher. She also knew how to paddle a canoe and what to do if the canoe tipped over. These skills earned Hillary a summer job with the parks department. She enjoyed giving water sports lessons to younger children.

Hillary's father seldom missed a chance to remind the children how fortunate they were. Once on a family visit to his hometown of Scranton, he took them to see a coal mine. The miners had hard, dangerous jobs. They worked underground in narrow tunnels, breathing dangerous coal dust. This, he told Hillary and her brothers, was the kind of work a lot of people had to do to survive. "It's a tough world out there," he reminded them.

Hillary and her brothers certainly didn't take money for granted. The Rodhams didn't try to keep up with Park Ridge's wealthiest families. They didn't belong to the country club, like the families of some of Hillary's classmates. Sometimes they even did without things that most other people took for granted. Their house was one of the last in Park Ridge to get a television set. But the family had so many other interests that they didn't really miss watching TV.

Sometimes Hugh Rodham could be a strict father. Hillary remembered once showing her report card to her dad. She was always near the top of her class, but this time she had done a little better than usual. The card was covered with A's. Her father didn't seem to be impressed. He set the card aside. "You must go to an easy school," he said. Later, as a grownup, Hillary could look back at this and laugh at her father's gruff ways. "Mr. Reality Check," she called him.

All three Rodham children did well in school, but Hugh and Tony were more easygoing than Hillary. They both loved sports and were not quite as interested in studying. Maybe the Rodhams expected a little more of Hillary because she was the oldest.

One thing her parents never told Hillary was that she should expect less of herself just because she was a girl. Dorothy Rodham was happy being a homemaker, but at times she thought about what it would have been like to attend college and have a career. She thought it was very important for girls to be independent. "No daughter of mine was going to have to go through the agony of being afraid to say what was on her mind," she said.

Hillary grew up assuming that all girls were given as much encouragement as she got at home. She was so used to competing with boys that she was surprised to learn that some people did think there were limits to what a girl could do.

In 1960, when Hillary was thirteen, John F. Kennedy was elected president. The space program was one of his great interests. The Soviet Union had already sent up the first satellite into space. President Kennedy was determined that the American space program would catch up to the Soviets' and become the best in the world. He made putting an astronaut on the moon a national goal.

Although science wasn't her favorite subject, Hillary got excited about the idea of becoming an astronaut. She wrote a letter to the National Aeronautics and Space Administration (NASA), the agency in charge of the space program. How could she prepare for astronaut training? she asked. What courses should she take? Some days later a letter from NASA arrived in the mail. It was very brief: "We are not accepting girls for astronaut training," it said.

Hillary thought it was terribly unfair that only boys could enter the space program. Later on, she would learn that astronauts had to have nearly perfect vision. Since she was very nearsighted, she couldn't have been an astronaut anyway. This made her feel a little better.

After learning that women couldn't be astronauts, Hillary began to think about other careers. Maybe she would become a doctor. Or a lawyer. But she was almost fifteen now, and she had begun to notice that some of her girlfriends weren't thinking about careers. All they seemed to think about was boys and clothes and makeup.

"I saw a lot of my friends who were doing well in school beginning to worry that boys would think they were too smart," she said. These girls stopped asking questions in class because they worried that boys didn't like smart girls. Instead of taking courses they were interested in, they planned their class schedules so that they could be around certain boys they liked.

"Gosh—why are they doing that?" Hillary wondered. She liked boys too, but she couldn't see changing who she was in order to be popular.

More and more when Hillary's girlfriends got together, they spent their time listening to records and talking about boys, makeup, and clothes. Hillary liked the rock-and-roll part. Among her favorite performers were Frankie Avalon and Fabian, two teen idols who were as famous for their good looks as for their music. And Hillary didn't mind talking about boys in her class, either. But she found it hard to share her friends' total interest in clothes and makeup.

"When she was fifteen or sixteen and the other kids were starting to use makeup, she wasn't interested," Hillary's mother remembered. "That used to annoy me a little bit. I used to think, Why can't she put on a little makeup?"

Actually Hillary didn't have much reason to worry about her looks. She had blue eyes and dimples that became even deeper when she smiled. Her light brown hair was shiny and healthy looking. And though her classmates didn't consider her beautiful, she was pretty, with a lot of personality.

Still, Hillary had one complaint about her appearance—her eyesight. Most girls will find one thing about their appearance that bothers them. Hillary's complaint was the same problem that would have made it impossible for her to become an astronaut. Ever since grade school she had worn "Coke bottle" eyeglasses, glasses with lenses so thick they look like the heavy bottoms of soda bottles.

Hillary hated her glasses. When she was to have her picture taken, she usually took them off. Sometimes she tried to do without them in the halls at school. Her friends teased her about being unable to see what was going on.

When it came to clothes, it was probably a good thing that Hillary wasn't too style conscious. As far as her father was concerned the time to buy new clothes was when her old ones were completely worn out. Even then he had to be persuaded.

"Dad, I *really* need a new pair of shoes," Hillary would plead. "These have holes in them."

"Have you done your chores?"

After the chores were all done, he would reluctantly reach into his wallet and give her the money she needed for shoes or clothes.

Her father's strictness must have been hard at times. But as she grow older, Hillary realized that her parents had given her something more important than clothes. They had taught her to set her own goals and not to be too dependent on other people's opinions of her. "I never felt anything but support from my family," she said. "Whatever I thought I could do and be, they supported."

A Wider World

In spite of her father's lectures about hard times, Hillary knew very little about the world outside Park Ridge. She thought that other places were like her own community, safe and comfortable. But when she was fourteen, she met an adult who would encourage her to broaden her horizons. While many of her girlfriends at school were focusing on boys and dating, she was beginning to learn about the wider world outside her hometown.

The Rodham family had always attended the First United Methodist Church in Park Ridge. First United Methodist was a large church. There were more than a hundred eleven- and twelve-year-olds in Hillary's confirmation class! With so many members the congregation could afford a full-time youth minister to organize programs for the young people.

When Hillary was a freshman in high school, Don Jones became the church's new youth minister. Jones was just out of theology school and full of enthusiasm. He was eager to introduce the teenagers in the youth group to new ideas and experiences. With Jones in charge the group's Thursday night meetings became exciting. He sometimes called the group the "University of Life."

The new minister arranged showings of foreign movies that were unlikely to be seen at the local movie house. He introduced the teenagers to folksingers like Bob Dylan. He made them aware of protest music, popular music that raises questions about problems in the world. He also encouraged the group to discuss books and religion. Faith isn't just a personal thing, he often said. True Christians also have to be committed to making the world a better place.

Once Jones invited an atheist to come to a meeting and explain why he didn't believe in God. Another meeting was about the problem of teenage pregnancy. Some of these topics were controversial with the adults in the church. They thought that teenagers were too young to be hearing about such things. Of course, their strict attitude only made the meetings more popular with the kids.

Although Park Ridge is a suburb of Chicago, there were large farms just a short drive away. Every year migrant workers were brought in from other parts of the country, and even from outside the country, to pick crops. Don Jones took the kids to see the shacks where the migrant workers and their families lived. The church group learned that the workers often had to leave their younger children while they worked in the fields. Jones's group made it their project to send the older teenagers out to the camp to baby-sit.

Hillary got involved with raising money to pay for the baby-sitting project. She organized fund-raisers, such as a neighborhood sports tournament. Hillary thought working on these events was fun. She never had trouble getting others involved. Dorothy Rodham was proud of the way Hillary took charge. "Mothers in the neighborhood were amazed at how they couldn't get their boys to do much," she said, "but Hillary had them all running around."

Park Ridge didn't have any black families at the time, and most of the kids in town had never seen a really poor neighborhood. Jones took his group to Chicago's inner city, where they met African-American and Hispanic teenagers. The minister would use music or even a painting as a starting point to get the kids talking to each other.

At one meeting Jones showed up with a copy of *Guernica,* a painting by Pablo Picasso about the terrors of war. He asked everyone what they saw in the picture. To the kids from Park Ridge, *Guernica* was only a painting. But for some of the inner-city teenagers it had a personal message. The city teens talked about people in their own families who had been robbed or shot.

The kids from the city may have had very different experiences from the suburban kids. But the two groups also learned that they had a lot in common. They realized that teenagers everywhere have problems with parents and schoolwork. They sometimes worry about what their classmates think of them and how to fit in with the group.

During those years civil rights was in the news almost every night. In the American South, segregation was the law. Segregation meant that African-Americans were to be kept separate from whites in many public places. Black people had to sit in the back of the buses and in special sections in movie theaters. Many restaurants refused to serve them. And in public buildings certain rest rooms and even drinking fountains were set aside for use by whites only.

Martin Luther King, Jr., was a civil rights leader who fought for the rights of African-Americans during the time Hillary was growing up. He led many demonstrations to overturn segregation. He preached a philosophy of nonviolence. That meant that demonstrators didn't fight back even when the police sent attack dogs against them. But when Americans turned on their TVs for the evening news and saw how brutally the peaceful demonstrators were treated, they were ashamed. As a result one city after another made segregation illegal.

In the spring of 1962, near the end of Hillary's freshman year, Martin Luther King, Jr., came to Chicago. One Sunday evening Don Jones took Hillary and the rest of the Park Ridge youth group into the city to hear Dr. King make a speech. Afterward he made sure the group had a chance to meet Dr. King and shake hands with him.

Meeting Dr. King was one of the high points of Hillary's life. By this time she had learned that there were many evils in the world. Don Jones had taught her youth group about poverty and prejudice. And her teachers in school talked about the threat of nuclear war. Still, people like Dr. King were working hard to solve these problems. Knowing that, Hillary and her friends had a sense of hope and confidence about the future.

But all that would change a year and a half later.

A Turning Point

November 22, 1963, started out as an ordinary day for Hillary and the rest of the junior class at Maine East High School. But by midday a rumor had begun to circulate. A few students had heard that the president of the United States had been shot. During class changeovers everyone was talking about the rumor. Some kids were upset. A few were in tears. Still others refused to believe it. They were sure that this was one of those wild stories that somehow grow and grow until people begin to take them seriously.

Then there was an announcement. The principal called an emergency assembly. Filing into the auditorium, the students began to realize that the rumor must be true. Soon the principal confirmed their fears. President Kennedy was dead. His body was already on Air Force One, the presidential airplane, being flown back to Washington. The vice president, Lyndon Johnson, had taken the president's oath of office.

Hillary and her friends were in a daze. "It hadn't occurred to us that presidents got shot," Hillary later said.

Hillary would remember that day as the "absolute turning point" in her life. It wasn't so much that John

Kennedy, the Democratic president, had been her hero. In fact, her parents were Republicans. But for Hillary and other young people of the time, the assassination was a terrible shock. For the first time they realized how quickly things can change. One minute the president had been so young and full of life. The next he was gone. Hillary and others of her generation no longer felt confident that the world was getting better. They wondered what bad thing would happen next.

The Kennedy assassination made Hillary a more serious person. Don Jones had left Park Ridge earlier that fall to continue his education. But Hillary kept in touch, writing him long, thoughtful letters. She was beginning to think about her future. More and more she felt that she ought to go into public service.

Hillary was also becoming more interested in politics. A presidential election was coming up in November 1964, the fall of her senior year. When her parents talked about the campaign at dinner, she paid close attention.

The Rodhams had always discussed current affairs at home. Hugh Rodham was a Republican, and a conservative one at that. Dorothy Rodham sometimes sided with the Democrats, but not very loudly. Hugh Rodham was very excited about the Republican candidate, Barry Goldwater. And so was Hillary.

That September, Hillary and her classmates transferred to Maine South, a larger regional high school. Mr. Baker, the government teacher at Maine South, organized a mock election. Hillary and a girl named Ellen Murdoch were chosen to represent the candidates. Just as Hillary was all for Goldwater, Ellen was enthusiastic about the Democrat, Lyndon Johnson.

But Mr. Baker had a surprise. "Hillary, you'll try to persuade the students to vote for Johnson," he said. "Ellen will give the speech for Goldwater."

Both girls were outraged. They couldn't believe it. But Mr. Baker told them that they already knew the arguments for their own candidates. They would learn a lot more from trying to put themselves in their opponent's shoes.

On the day of the assembly Hillary gave a forceful speech, urging her fellow students to vote for Lyndon Johnson. The majority voted for Goldwater anyway. Most families in Park Ridge were loyal Republicans. Hillary must have had mixed feelings about the vote. She was really for Goldwater, but she had been trying to persuade the students to vote for Johnson. She learned how hard it is to give a speech that will persuade people to change their minds.

The mock election wasn't the only vote that went against Hillary that year. She ran for senior-class president and lost. Still, she had a very busy schedule. She worked on the school newspaper and belonged to the Pep Club. She served on the student council and was a member of the National Honor Society.

All these activities, plus studying to keep up an A average, didn't leave much time for dating. But like many other teenagers, Hillary and her friends thought about romance and adventure. A few years earlier the Pickfair Theater had shown a movie called *Where the Boys Are*. It was a musical about a group of girls who go to Florida during spring vacation and fall in love. By today's standards the movie was old-fashioned. But to Hillary and her friends a trip to Florida sounded thrilling. It was all they could talk about.

After saying no many times, the girls' parents finally gave in and okayed a spring-vacation trip to Florida. But they insisted that the group take along an adult chaperone, a young woman teacher.

The girls had high hopes for the trip. Each of them dreamed of meeting someone special. As it turned out the first people they met on the beach were another group of girls who lived near Park Ridge!

Of all the girls in the group, it was Hillary who attracted boys. One evening she let a boy walk her back to her hotel. They stayed up late talking. When she came inside, she found her roommate in tears—she felt left out. Hillary realized that if she kept seeing the boy, her friends who hadn't met anyone would be miserable and maybe a little angry with her. Romance in real life was a lot more complicated than in the movies!

The Florida trip didn't turn out to be the great adventure all the girls had hoped for, but Hillary did have opportunities to date back home in Park Ridge. Although she got along well with the boys in her class, most of the boys she went out with were a few years older. It may have been that boys her age were a little timid about asking out a girl who was so smart and confident. But those same qualities attracted young men who were already in college. One boy she dated was a Princeton student, home on vacation.

Hillary's parents discouraged her from getting too

involved with any boy. They told all their children to have fun with their friends but to put off serious relationships until they were older.

When it came time to pick a college, Hillary considered a number of schools. She had heard about Wellesley from a student teacher who had gone there. Wellesley was an excellent school. It was also all-female and on the East Coast, in Massachusetts, farther from home than most of her friends were going. On impulse Hillary filled out an application. With her good grades and many accomplishments, it was no surprise that she was accepted. Hillary's college choice was set.

Soon high school graduation day arrived. Hillary wasn't quite first in her class but she had finished in the top five percent. She had been a National Merit finalist and an honor student. Her classmates had also voted her "the girl most likely to succeed." At the commencement ceremony her name was called so many times for awards and prizes that even her proud mother felt "a little embarrassed," as she put it.

Some of Hillary's classmates thought she was brave to be going to Wellesley. It was hundreds of miles from home, and she wouldn't know anyone there. In fact, Hillary was a little nervous about her decision. She had been to a few gatherings given for Chicago-area girls who were thinking of attending women's colleges in the East. The hostesses all appeared to be wealthy women. Their surroundings usually were rich and fancy. Hillary wasn't sure she would fit in with girls from homes like these. Still, Wellesley offered an opportunity to get a first-class education. She decided to take her chances.

To College in the Sixties

In the fall of 1965 Hillary Rodham arrived at Wellesley with at least a touch of nervousness—and a proper wardrobe of pleated skirts, white blouses, and kneesocks. She was used to wearing conservative clothes in quiet Park Ridge. Hillary planned to major in political science and become a lawyer—and she did stick to her goal. But in the meantime the world was changing all around her.

The middle years of the 1960s were a time of turmoil in many areas of American life. The civil rights protests in the South had shown college students that demonstrations were a powerful way to get attention. In the protests hundreds of people would gather and demand changes in the way blacks were treated. They would march through the streets chanting and carrying signs that stated their demand for equal rights. On college campuses too, students had begun to organize marches and student strikes. Some of the marches were protests against segregation; others were against sending American soldiers to fight in Vietnam. But students also wanted changes in the way colleges treated students.

Young people entering college around the time Hillary did had been born soon after the end of World

War II. So many babies were born in those years that the period became known as the "baby boom." Now, in the mid-1960s, colleges everywhere were crowded with these young people, called baby boomers. This generation had grown up with television. Its members knew a lot about the world. They felt that many college rules were out of date. They wanted changes in the way they were taught too. Since there were so many students, they were able to make themselves heard.

As a Wellesley freshman Hillary started the year by joining the campus Republican Club. At the time, however, most students who were active in politics were Democrats. The Republican Club had very few members. Hillary soon found herself elected president.

But Hillary was also attracted to the more radical students, the Democrats. It was these students who wanted to use politics for social change. Hillary soon became part of a group on campus that loved to sit around the table after meals and debate political issues.

At the time Wellesley had fewer than a dozen African-American students. In the dormitories they almost always roomed together, not by choice but because the administration segregated them. When the minority students called on the college to change this policy, Hillary supported them. She also protested against curfews in the dorms and the rule against students having male visitors in their rooms.

By the end of her freshman year Hillary's pleated skirts and kneesocks were gone. When she returned home to Park Ridge for summer vacation, she wore long print skirts and rimless granny glasses. One day she happened to run into one of her high school teachers, Mr. Paul Carlson. He was amazed at the change. "Hillary's gone radical on us," he told his family.

Hugh Rodham was not at all happy about the change in his daughter. He complained that Wellesley was turning Hillary into a Democrat. Had he known that would happen, he asserted, he never would have let her go there!

But how much had Hillary really changed?

At Maine South High School, Hillary had agreed with most of her fellow students on the issues. And even at Wellesley she was still "middle of the road." The most "radical" thing Hillary did in her freshman year was invite an African-American student to attend services at an all-white church in town. Afterward some of Hillary's friends criticized her. They wondered if she wasn't just trying to get attention. Hillary didn't think so, but she was worried enough to write to her old youth group director, Don Jones, for advice. She later admitted that she was probably testing her own courage to be different.

Many of Hillary's friends at Wellesley were government and social science majors. They were more serious than the average student. Hillary remembered sitting around a table while they discussed Wellesley's official motto: Not to be ministered unto but to minister. They debated what the motto meant in their own lives. How much time should be devoted to doing things for others? How much difference could one person make? "As students," Hillary would recall, "we debated passionately what responsibility each individual has for the larger society."

The summer after her sophomore year, as part of a program for government majors, Hillary worked in Washington, D.C. She was a student intern in the office of the congressman who represented her hometown of Park Ridge. The congressman Hillary worked for happened to be a Republican. But by the spring of 1968, in her junior year, Hillary did what her father had most feared. She became a Democrat. She campaigned for Eugene McCarthy, the antiwar candidate, who was running against President Lyndon Johnson in the primaries.

That April there was another shocking assassination. Martin Luther King, Jr., was shot to death in Tennessee. Dr. King's death left many students angry and frustrated. He had taught nonviolence, but he died a victim of violence. Some Wellesley students felt they needed to do something dramatic to show how upset they were. They talked about boycotting classes or even staging a sit-down strike in the president's office. The students held an emotional meeting, with lots of shouting and confusion.

After a while Hillary was asked to run the meeting. Soon the group was on its way to making a decision. They decided to organize a teach-in, a special series of classes. For one day there would be meetings and discussions about Dr. King's life and work. Students could attend these events instead of their regular classes. The teach-in would give them a chance to learn about Dr. King and to talk about their feelings.

Hillary often wound up playing the role of moderator, running meetings. She was a good listener. She could understand when people were upset and emotional. But she had little patience with people who just wanted to talk about how angry they were. Hillary was often the one who tried to get people to stop discussing the problem and start talking about solutions.

In her four years at Wellesley, Hillary devoted thousands of hours to student committees. A lot of her time was spent on the kind of work that other students found boring and unglamorous. As a senior she was elected president of the student government. And she also found time to keep up an A average in her courses.

But even with her studies and the many organizations she belonged to, Hillary's life at Wellesley wasn't all work. She liked to dance to the music of then-popular groups such as the Beatles and the Supremes. She went out on dates, though she had no really serious boyfriends. When she had time, she liked to go to the gym and do exercises for an hour or so. Many of her friends thought exercise was a strange hobby!

While in college Hillary became more relaxed than she had been in high school. She sometimes wore attention-getting clothes, such as striped pants and jangling jewelry. She even broke a few rules. One of her "favorite rules to break" was the ban on swimming in Lake Waban, on the Wellesley campus.

The year Hillary graduated from Wellesley, 1969, members of the senior class decided they wanted to make a change in the commencement ceremony. Usually commencement speakers were guests from outside the college. They received honorary degrees and made speeches, giving the students advice. But this year some of the seniors thought they should have a voice in their commencement too. A group of students asked Hillary if she would be the one to represent them.

At first the dean refused the students' request. Then, just a few days before the ceremony, the dean changed her mind. The students in the group got together to help Hillary write her speech. They made lots of suggestions. One girl even wrote a short poem!

Hillary's place on the program was immediately after the principal guest speaker, Senator Edward Brooke. The senator gave the kind of speech that graduates all over America were hearing that June. He gently criticized student protesters and defended President Nixon's policies, which were unpopular with many students.

The senator was sincere. Maybe he was even right about some things. But some students felt that he was talking down to them, as if the protesters were children throwing tantrums. He didn't seem to understand how serious they were.

When Senator Brooke finished his speech, Hillary was introduced. Walking up to the podium, she stared out at her classmates and their families. Dressed in her commencement robe and her usual thick eyeglasses, she looked small and alone. But Hillary was used to speaking up for herself. She decided that she couldn't let the moment slip by.

Setting aside her typed speech, Hillary tried to answer the senator's criticism. She had a few criticisms of him too. She said his thinking was out-of-date—"irrelevant" to the problems of the day.

Hillary spoke from her heart for about ten minutes. Then she picked up her prepared speech and started to read. In this part of her talk she tried to describe the feelings of the young people of her generation. Just aiming for a career in business, a big house, and a new car wasn't enough for them. They felt very strongly that America was on the brink of a "great adventure," a great "experiment in human living," as she called it.

Her generation, she went on, expected more from government. "The challenge now is to practice politics as the art of making what appears to be impossible, possible."

These were fine words. But what did they mean? In fact, many young people at the time thought that it would indeed be possible to wipe out poverty in America in a few short years. They even thought they could end war and racism. They really believed they could succeed where past generations had failed.

Looking back on her speech twenty-five years later, Hillary would admit she had no idea then how hard it is to change the world. Even small victories take a lot of work. But maybe it wasn't such a bad thing to have so much hope. "I'm glad I felt like that when I was twenty-one," she said.

That day in June when Hillary finished speaking, some members of her class stood and cheered. But not everyone was pleased. Many people thought the ideas in her speech were immature. She never really said what her generation would do to make the world a better place. And some older graduates of the college thought she had been rude to Senator Brooke. The senator himself was understanding. He said he didn't take Hillary's criticism personally.

In the end Hillary Rodham's speech got a lot of attention. It even made her famous in a small way. *Life* magazine chose Hillary and two other graduation speakers from other colleges to represent the voices of the sixties generation. Her picture appeared in the magazine, along with some parts of her speech.

But by the time commencement day was over, Hillary was just relieved to have the experience behind her. That evening she wanted to do something a little bit wild to celebrate her last day at college. When night fell, she sneaked out to the shore of Lake Waban. Stripping down to her bathing suit, she left her clothes in a neat pile and went for a swim.

Unfortunately while she was in the water, a security guard came along. He didn't notice Hillary in the lake. Or at least he didn't challenge her to come out. But he did pick up the pile of clothing she had left on the shore. After her swim Hillary waded out of the lake and began searching for her eyeglasses. The guard had taken them too!

Without her glasses Hillary was lost—"Blind as a bat," she said later. "I had to *feel* my way back to my room." Luckily no one else saw her. It would have been embarrassing for the student commencement speaker to be discovered staggering around campus after dark wearing nothing but her bathing suit.

That summer Hillary had a chance to travel. She went to Alaska and found a summer job. But her break from studying didn't last long. In the fall she would begin her first year at Yale University Law School in New Haven, Connecticut.

Yale University has one of the top law schools in the country. Just getting into Yale Law is a big step on the path to success.

But in 1969 female law students weren't as common as they are today. While at Wellesley, Hillary had been interested in going to law school at Harvard. Someone introduced her to a professor from Harvard. He told her, "We don't need any more women at Harvard Law." Hillary decided to go to Yale instead.

Hillary was one of just thirty women in Yale Law's class of 1972. In most classes there were dozens of male students and only a few female. Some professors thought it was a waste of time for women to go to law school. They thought that when a woman got married, she would probably quit work anyway.

Of the thirty women in Hillary's class, ten dropped out before graduation. The ratio of men to women became even bigger. But Hillary wasn't one to sit and worry about feeling out of place. Her family had taught her to focus on her goals. She became one of the leaders of her class.

Most of the students in the law school were working hard to prepare for their future careers. But by the spring semester of Hillary's first year at Yale, the wave of student protests all over America had caught up with them. In the early sixties the student demonstrations against the Vietnam War had been peaceful. But now, as the 1970s began, the mood had changed. On two campuses, Kent State in Ohio and Jackson State in Mississippi, demonstrators were shot and killed. Some of the more radical students had begun to see the police and even college officials as the enemy. There was talk of violence and revolution.

In the city of New Haven, at a courthouse not far from the Yale campus, members of the Black Panther party were on trial for murder. The Panthers were a small group of black radicals. The Panthers talked about revolution. They had declared war on the police. To some people in the student movement, the Panthers were heroes. Most of the men and women at Yale Law didn't feel that way, but they did wonder if the judge and jury would be able to keep an open mind. Even the president of Yale had said he wasn't sure the trial would be fair.

One of Hillary's law school classes made the trial its special project. They went to court and collected as much information as they could.

Before long the trial led to talk of a student strike in all the schools at Yale. Just as at Wellesley there was an angry meeting, and Hillary once again found herself trying to keep order. She succeeded. But she also found that working for compromise can be a thankless job. For a while some people on both sides saw her as the enemy.

For a few short months students across America were talking about revolution. Then, as quickly as the excitement began, things turned sour. At Yale the change happened sooner than in most places. The evidence against the Panthers was stronger than most students had expected. They were convicted. Meanwhile, there was a fire in one of the libraries on campus. Most people thought the fire had been set on purpose. Students were shocked. This wasn't at all the kind of change they wanted.

In the spring of 1970 Hillary heard a speech by a woman graduate of the law school. Marian Wright Edelman had gone on from Yale to become the first black woman lawyer in the state of Mississippi. Edelman talked about using the law to help poor people, especially children. Her organization, the Children's Defense Fund, was looking for ways to help the children of migrant farmworkers.

After the speech Hillary went up to Ms. Edelman and asked for a job.

"I'm sorry," Edelman told her. "We'd love to have you. But we just don't have the money."

For most job seekers that would have been the end of it. Not for Hillary. She got Marian Edelman to promise that she would hire her if Hillary could find someone else to pay her salary. She began to make phone calls and write letters. Eventually she found a group that would give her a kind of work scholarship. Then she called the Children's Defense Fund and told Marian Edelman the good news: "I'm coming to work for you."

Hillary spent the summer talking to migrant workers. She learned that many families lived in shacks. The children moved from school to school. Sometimes they worked in the fields instead of going to class.

When she returned to Yale in the fall, Hillary knew what she wanted to do. She took special courses in child psychology. She even arranged to spend an extra year in law school, studying at the Yale Child Study Center. She wanted to become an expert in the way the law treats children.

As a teenager Hillary had visited migrant workers' camps with her church group. She never forgot the children she saw there. Now she was planning a career that would make it possible for her to help other children like them.

The Man from Arkansas

Hillary worked hard at Yale. But her life at Yale wasn't all work. She liked to go out with friends for milk shakes. She still liked to dance. She dated several fellow students. But so far, she hadn't found anyone she considered really special. That would change when she was twenty-four and in her second year at New Haven.

One day while Hillary was studying in the library, she noticed that a good-looking young man was watching her.

Finally she closed her books and walked across the room to where he was sitting.

"If you're going to keep staring at me and I'm going to keep staring at you, we might as well know each other's name. I'm Hillary Rodham."

Her new acquaintance just grinned. He was so taken by surprise that he couldn't even remember his name. It was Bill Clinton.

Bill Clinton has always loved to tell the story of this meeting. "I was so embarrassed," he says. "But we've been together more or less ever since."

Hillary remembers that day too. But she points out that she already knew who Bill Clinton was. She had seen him one day in a student lounge. Another time, before the day she introduced herself in the library, he had started talking to her while she was standing in line to register for a course. When they got to the head of the line, it turned out that Bill was already registered. Hillary concluded that Bill had joined the line to talk to her, even if he didn't admit it.

Bill Clinton was a first-year student at the law school, a year behind Hillary, but he was actually a year older. As a senior in college he had won a Rhodes scholarship, one of the most important honors awarded to undergraduates. Winners of this scholarship get to spend two years studying at Oxford University in England. Now Bill was back in America and just starting law school.

Many young men would have made a point of talking about their experiences at Oxford. Instead, Bill Clinton preferred to brag about his home state of Arkansas. He talked about how beautiful it was, and how friendly.

But Arkansas was also the second-poorest state in the nation. Bill's own family often had trouble making ends meet. His mother had worked as a nurse to support the family.

When he was a junior in high school, Bill had attended a summer camp in Arkansas called Boys' State. As a way to learn about government the campers ran a mock election. Bill ran for "senator" and won. He and the other winners got to attend a national Boys' State convention in Washington, D.C. As part of the visit they were invited to the White House, where Bill shook hands with President Kennedy. It was a moment that would change his life. Now Bill's goal was to go to law school, return home after he finished, and get into politics. He wanted to help solve his state's many problems. He also had dreams of someday becoming president of the United States.

Bill Clinton was one of those students who seem to get A's without ever cracking a book. Friendly and outgoing, he loved to meet new people. Hillary wasn't exactly shy; she had proved that when she introduced herself to him in the library. But most of the time she was a more reserved, quiet person. In her free time she relaxed and had fun with people she knew well. Hillary's friends thought she liked being around Bill because of his sense of humor. He could always make her laugh. For his part, Bill was proud to have a girl-friend who was a leader on campus.

Bill and Hillary soon became a law school team. Together they presented a case in moot court, a kind of pretend trial where law students argue cases. They lost the case, but they enjoyed the experience of working together on something they cared about.

In the summer of 1972 they both went to Texas to work on the campaign of the Democratic presidential candidate, George McGovern. Even though McGovern didn't win, Bill and Hillary learned a lot about how an election campaign works. And even though they missed weeks of classes, Bill and Hillary still got A's on their first-semester exams. Their friends were amazed at the accomplishments of this bright and active couple.

That same year Bill Clinton also visited Park Ridge to meet Hillary's family. He enjoyed talking to Dorothy Rodham about a philosophy course she was taking. He helped do chores around the house. He even joined in the family card games. The Rodhams often made up their own rules to their favorite games. Bill mastered them all. By the end of the weekend he had been accepted almost as a member of the family.

Things were fine at the moment. But what about the future?

In the early 1970s very few women ran for national office. But quite a few of Hillary's friends and teachers predicted that she would become a congresswoman, a senator, or maybe even the first woman president. Bill Clinton said later that he was almost afraid to fall in love with Hillary. He wondered if she could be happy as the wife of a politician in a small state.

Still, he did fall in love. When he thought about marriage, he couldn't picture himself sharing his life with anyone else. He told his mother, "I want you to pray for me that it's Hillary, because if it isn't Hillary, it's nobody."

Hillary insisted that she never wanted to run for office. But she did want to work in government, or in a job where she could play a role in influencing policy. Her parents had sacrificed to help her get an excellent education. And Hillary had worked hard to prepare for a career in children's law. There weren't a great many jobs in this specialized field. And most of the jobs that existed would be in Washington, D.C., or some other big city. If she gave all that up for marriage, wouldn't that prove that the people who said women didn't belong at Yale and Harvard were right?

Because Hillary had decided to spend an extra year

40

studying children and family law, she finished law school at Yale in 1973, the same year as Bill. After graduation Bill packed his bags and went home. He would be teaching law at the University of Arkansas, in Fayetteville.

Hillary went to work in Boston for the Children's Defense Fund. One of her projects was to find out how many children in America weren't enrolled in school. Since high school she had known that the children of migrant farmworkers often miss a lot of classes. She was surprised to find how many other boys and girls weren't in school either. Many of them were disabled. Some had been expelled and no school would take them. Others were in the United States illegally. Their parents kept them out of school because they didn't want the authorities to catch them.

While Hillary was settling into her new job, the whole country was talking about the Watergate scandal. Workers for President Nixon's 1972 campaign had been accused of being dishonest during the campaign.

Now a committee of Congress was investigating whether President Nixon had lied about knowing of the Watergate break-in. Hillary was offered a chance to work in Washington as a staff attorney for the committee.

It was too exciting an opportunity to turn down. In January 1974, after just six months in Boston, Hillary went to work in Washington. Her new job was to do legal research for the committee. Forty-three young attorneys were on the staff. Only three of them were women.

Part of Hillary's job was listening to the famous secret tape recordings that Nixon had made in the Oval Office. But the work wasn't always this interesting, and the hours were long. The staff was often in the office until nine or ten at night. "The only way we knew it was weekends was because people would change from ties to jeans," said a male lawyer who worked with Hillary.

The staff attorneys weren't allowed to talk about their work, even to friends. And it was hard to keep refusing to answer the questions that everyone asked them wherever they went. So when the staff did have time to socialize, they did things together.

Even with these disadvantages it was an exciting job for a first-year lawyer. The committee had voted to impeach President Nixon. When a president is impeached, he has to stand trial in the Senate. The senators can vote to remove him from office. Only one president has ever been impeached—that was Andrew Johnson in 1868, after the Civil War. (He was acquitted, or found not guilty.) For several months it looked as though Nixon would be the second president to be impeached. The staff felt that they were part of history in the making.

Then in August 1974 President Nixon announced that he was resigning. Suddenly Hillary's work in Washington was finished.

Hillary had always known the job would be temporary. She just hadn't expected it to end quite so soon. In the fourteen months since she graduated from law school, she had kept in touch with Bill Clinton by phone and letters. His feelings about her hadn't changed at all. He kept urging her to think about moving to Arkansas.

Now, at twenty-eight, Bill was running in his first major campaign, as a candidate for Congress. Since Hillary had some free time, she decided to go down to visit Bill in Fayetteville and help out. Her two brothers, Hugh and Tony, went with her.

Hillary and her brothers helped organize Bill's race for Congress. In the end, he didn't win. But he came close. It was a good first try for a young man barely out of law school.

In between tacking up campaign posters and making phone calls Hillary looked around for work. She was offered a job teaching in the law school of the University of Arkansas. It was a good job, but Hillary wasn't sure she wanted to take it.

As nice as the state of Arkansas might be, it was strange territory to Hillary Rodham. She was a city girl. Later she said humorously that "like many people who grew up in Chicago," she "didn't even know where Arkansas was."

What Hillary saw of Fayetteville during her visit didn't reassure her. The people she met were friendly. The law students were even excited about having a teacher who had played a role, however small, in the Watergate investigation. But Fayetteville seemed very small compared to Washington.

Moving to Arkansas also meant that she wouldn't be able to return to work for the Children's Defense Fund. Hillary wasn't even sure what kind of opportunities there were for women lawyers in the state.

She didn't want to teach law forever; she wanted to work as a lawyer too.

Many of Hillary's friends thought she would be making a big mistake by moving to Fayetteville. Even Hillary's mother was worried. "What kind of sacrifices are you supposed to make for love?" she remembered asking. "I wondered if Arkansas would be so great for Hillary."

When faced with a decision, Hillary has always looked for a compromise. But this time there was no middle way. As she put it, "I decided to follow my heart."

Marriage and Motherhood

Even though Hillary was following her heart to Arkansas, she wasn't making any snap decisions. She planned to find her own apartment in Fayetteville. She would make an independent life for herself in her new home. If that worked out, she could make the more important decision about marrying Bill Clinton.

Still, the move to Arkansas was a big step. Hillary didn't even own a car. She went back to Washington to pack her things, and a girlfriend named Sara volunteered to drive her back to Arkansas. The two of them packed her belongings into ten cardboard boxes and loaded them into the back of Sara's car.

During the long drive Sara tried to keep a positive attitude. But in her own mind she was afraid Hillary was making a big mistake. Every so often she would blurt out what she was really thinking. "You're going to end up married to a country lawyer," she warned.

Hillary wasn't so much worried about Bill Clinton. But she did wonder if she could be happy in a place where she didn't know anyone else. Would she miss big-city life and the excitement of a job where she could play a role in national issues?

It turned out that Hillary did have some familiar company when she moved. Her brother Hugh had recently returned from the Peace Corps. He enrolled at the University of Arkansas, where Hillary was teaching, and moved to Arkansas. They found a small apartment together. Since Hillary had never taught before, she had to spend many hours planning her courses. She also found it surprisingly easy to make new friends. Arkansas was "warm and welcoming," she said. Before she knew it, the year was almost up.

Bill was getting impatient. He wanted her to make a decision about marriage. When he drove past a house with a FOR SALE sign on the lawn, he would think about living there with Hillary. One day he pointed out one of these houses to her. It was a small brick home, next to a lake. Hillary agreed that it was pretty.

Not long afterward Hillary went out of town on a short vacation. When she returned, Bill picked her up at the airport. The next thing she knew, they were parked in front of the little brick house. "Well," announced Bill, "you said you liked it, so I bought it. I guess now we'll have to get married."

This time Hillary agreed.

The wedding date was set for October 11, 1975. In the weeks before the wedding Hillary was busier than ever. The new house needed a lot of work before it would be ready to live in. She was teaching a full schedule of courses. And since her parents lived far away, she had to plan the wedding herself.

At last it was the day before the wedding. Her parents arrived from Illinois. Late in the afternoon Mrs.

Rodham asked if she could see her daughter's wedding dress.

"I didn't get around to buying one," Hillary answered.

Dorothy Rodham was shocked. She and her daughter piled into the car and raced downtown. By this time only one department store was still open. Hillary looked over the racks and found a linen dress that she liked.

Mrs. Rodham told this story with amazement. How could any woman forget to buy her own wedding dress? But Hillary's friends weren't surprised. Hillary liked nice clothes. She just didn't like to shop. Somehow, there were always other things she'd rather be doing.

Bill and Hillary even decided they were too busy to take time off. But Dorothy Rodham decided they needed a vacation. She bought tickets to Mexico. It was an unusual honeymoon. The rest of the Rodham family went along too!

Even though Bill Clinton had lost his race for Congress, he hadn't given up on politics. In 1976 he decided to run for attorney general of Arkansas. In that job he would be responsible for enforcing the laws of the state. That summer Bill ran in the Democratic primary election and won the right to be his party's candidate in the fall. He didn't have much to worry about after that. His Republican opponent was weak. Bill was almost sure to be elected in November.

As attorney general Bill would be working in the state capital, Little Rock. That meant selling the little

47

house by the lake just a year after he and Hillary had moved in. Hillary would also have to change careers again.

In the meantime Hillary was offered a chance to help organize Jimmy Carter's campaign for president against Gerald Ford. The job was in Indiana, but it would last for only a few months. Bill was busy with the campaign for attorney general, and it looked as if he was certain to win. Hillary decided to accept the job.

Putting together a political campaign is a big challenge. In just a few weeks the organizers have to rent offices, furnish them, and find a staff. They have to recruit volunteers who will reach voters all over the state. Everyone is under a lot of pressure. If the campaign doesn't go well, there can be arguments and hurt feelings. Hillary's strength was that she knew how to criticize people's work without hurting their feelings. "She never made you feel you were the problem," one campaign worker said.

There was also a lighter side to the Indiana campaign. The office that Hillary and her boss rented happened to be near the jail. One day the prisoners watched as a hundred telephones were installed in what looked like an empty office. Naturally they were curious. What was going on? The only thing they could think of was that someone was opening a place for taking illegal bets! The rumor reached the police, who started to plan a raid. Fortunately before that happened, they learned that the new office was Jimmy Carter's campaign headquarters.

Hillary later said that she learned a lot in Indiana.

48

In college she thought mostly about how government could do more things and do them better. During the campaign she saw that many workers weren't sure they wanted government to do more. They worried about high taxes and keeping their jobs.

After Jimmy Carter was elected, Hillary returned to Little Rock. In 1977 she joined the Rose Law Firm. At first her career was difficult. Women attorneys were still uncommon. Some of the judges weren't sure how to treat them. Once when she tried a criminal case, the judge didn't want her to listen to all the evidence. He thought some of it wasn't fit for a lady to hear!

In 1978 Bill Clinton ran for governor of Arkansas, the top job in the state. He was elected and took office the following year. At thirty-two he was the youngest governor in the country. The new First Lady of Arkansas was thirty-one. But the Clintons looked even younger than their age. Like many younger men in the seventies, Bill wore his hair a little long, with sideburns. Hillary still had long hair parted in the middle—and her thick glasses.

For the ball held to celebrate Bill's inauguration, Hillary did take time to order a special dress. She chose a long red gown, in a kind of soft velvet that was popular at the time. It was decorated with antique beads and lace that had been worn by women from some of the state's founding families. Hillary wanted her outfit for the ball to express her pride in her adopted state. Many people appreciated her attempt. But some complained that the new governor and his wife looked like hippie college students.

The argument over Hillary's dress was just the beginning of the Clintons' problems as governor and First Lady of Arkansas. People in the rest of the country often didn't have a high opinion of Arkansas. They thought of it as backward and poor. And the state did have many problems, including bad roads and poor schools. Bill Clinton took office with a long list of ideas for change. But these plans cost money. That meant raising taxes, and a lot of voters were very unhappy about being asked to pay more.

Some people in the state weren't even sure they wanted all the changes the governor had in mind. Arkansans did want more jobs and better schools. But a lot of them liked living in a place that was mainly rural. It seemed to them that Bill Clinton wanted to make Arkansas more like New York and California.

To Hillary's surprise, there were also people who were bothered by her name. After her marriage she had decided that she would still call herself Hillary Rodham. Many of her married classmates from Wellesley and Yale were keeping their maiden names. It seemed the practical thing to do. After all, she had already met hundreds of people in the legal field who knew her as Hillary Rodham. Being called Hillary Rodham, she told one reporter, made "me feel like a real person." She also had personal feelings about her name. She had worked hard to make her parents proud. Using the name Rodham was a way of saying thank you to them.

But to many people, especially older ones, the idea of a woman keeping her own name seemed strange. To them, it was a new custom that symbolized a lot of changes in American life, changes they weren't sure they liked. They wondered if Hillary thought her career was more important than her marriage.

One day at an office party Hillary found herself standing next to a stranger. She smiled politely and held out her hand. "How do you do?" she said. "I'm Hillary Rodham."

The man's face turned bright red. "No, you're not!" he screeched. "No, you're not!"

Hillary's name wasn't the only problem. In other ways she was having trouble fitting in. Of course, Hillary got dressed up when she went to the courtroom. But sometimes she would go into her law office wearing slacks and an old blouse. In Washington it wasn't that unusual for young lawyers to be so casual. But Little Rock was a much smaller city, and more conservative. People there weren't used to seeing women go to work in pants—especially not the governor's wife.

Even though she had little privacy—and a lot of challenges—as the state's First Lady, a lot of good things were happening in Hillary's life. In 1977 President Carter appointed her to the board of the Legal Services Corporation, a national organization that helped people who couldn't afford legal advice. She held other posts too. Governor Clinton appointed her to find ways to bring medical care to people in rural parts of Arkansas who lived far from the nearest doctor. And on her own Hillary started an organization that would study the needs of children in the state.

And then in late 1979 good news was officially announced. Hillary was going to have a baby.

Hillary loved children, and she and Bill always planned to have a family. Hillary wanted a home life like the close, supportive one she had known as a child. Becoming a father was important to Bill Clinton too, but for another reason. His own father died in an automobile accident a few months before he was born.

Bill Clinton once said that when he was a little boy, he used to think about what it would be like to have a father. "Oh, I imagined it all the time. I imagined what it would be like just to see him come around the corner at Christmastime." It meant a lot to him to know that even though he hadn't had his own dad around when he was growing up, he would get to be a dad to his child, to be with the child at Christmas and all the other important moments.

Motherhood should have been the easiest of all of Hillary's accomplishments. She ate right and didn't smoke. And she liked to exercise, long before fitness for women was in style. But in spite of her good health her pregnancy didn't go quite as planned. Hillary often didn't feel well.

One night in February she woke up in pain. An ambulance was called to the governor's house to rush her to the hospital. The doctors decided not to wait for the baby to be born by itself. They would perform an operation called a cesarean section and deliver the baby right away.

Bill Clinton insisted on going into the operating room with his wife. The doctors tried to talk him out of it. They were afraid he would faint. But he refused to change his mind. He wanted to see his baby being born.

The Clintons' daughter was born on February 27, 1980. Even though she had come a little early, she was a healthy baby.

One of the Clintons' favorite records was of Judy Collins singing a song popular at the time. "Wake Up, It's a Chelsea Morning!" It was happy, upbeat music. Bill suggested naming the baby after the song. Her full name would be Chelsea Victoria Clinton.

The Clintons were thrilled to be parents. Hillary took four months off from work to stay home with Chelsea. She was honest enough to admit that with all her education, she was a novice at the job of motherhood. Sometimes when Chelsea cried, she didn't know what to do.

One day, rocking the baby in her arms, she said to her, "Chelsea, you have never been a baby before, and I've never been a mother before. We are just going to have to help each other get through this together."

Marco Buscaglia/Maine East High School

Hillary Rodham, vice president of her junior class, stands with the other class officers at Maine East High School in Park Ridge, Illinois.

Marco Buscaglia/Maine East High School

Hillary in her senior year pictured with the other National Merit Scholarship finalists in her school.

54

Hillary grew up in this brick house on a quiet street in Park Ridge, Illinois.

Hillary and other members of the student council during her senior year.

Hillary's 1965 high school yearbook picture. Her classmates voted her "the girl most likely to succeed."

Courtesy Wellesley College Archives

*Hillary enjoyed
swimming in Lake
Waban while she
attended Wellesley
College, in
Massachusetts.*

Courtesy Wellesley College Archives

*Hillary Rodham
delivers the
commencement
speech at her college
graduation. She was
the first student at
Wellesley to be given
this honor.*

56

Lee Balterman/*Life* Magazine © Time Warner Inc.

Gottschalk/Sipa Press

This picture of Hillary appeared in Life magazine after her graduation speech. The magazine interviewed her and printed part of her speech.

As a law student at Yale University, Hillary presents a case in a mock trial.

Arkansas Democrat-Gazette

Hillary and Bill Clinton dance at the inaugural ball of 1979, when he was elected governor of Arkansas for his first term.

Arkansas Democrat-Gazette

Hillary looks on proudly as her husband is sworn in as governor of Arkansas.

Reuters/Bettmann

Sygma

Hillary and Bill Clinton hold their newborn baby daughter, Chelsea, who was born in 1980.

Hillary holding four-year-old Chelsea.

The Clintons attend a reception in Hillary's honor, with seven- year- old Chelsea.

Wesley Hitt/Gamma Liaison Network

AP/Wide World Photos

The First Lady and President Bill Clinton share a toast right after the inauguration ceremony made him the forty-second president of the United States.

59

AP/Wide World Photos

Hillary and Chelsea attend an inaugural ball given by MTV in celebration of Bill Clinton's election to the presidency.

AP/Wide World Photos

Hillary is surrounded by photographers before her testimony at the hearings on health-care reform. The First Lady was appointed head of the task force to improve health care for all Americans.

Don Perdue/CTW; Courtesy Children's Television Workshop

The First Lady takes time out of her busy schedule to appear on "Sesame Street" with Rosita and Big Bird.

61

First Lady Again

In November 1980 a Republican named Frank White ran against Bill Clinton for the governor's job. There were many issues in the campaign, including high taxes. But Frank White also talked a lot about Hillary Rodham's name. Over and over he told audiences, "My wife is proud to be known as Mrs. Frank White." He implied that Hillary wasn't proud to be married to her husband.

The voters chose the Republican candidate by a margin of almost thirty-two thousand votes. The loss was tough on Bill Clinton. For a while he felt that his political career was over. He wondered if he might not be happier as a country lawyer. The hardest part of it all was feeling that he had failed in his first important job of his life. "I knew at some point that I would have to run in 1982 in order to live with myself the rest of my life," he said.

Hillary encouraged her husband to learn from his mistakes and stay in politics. His decision to run again in the next election, in 1982, made them more of a team than ever. During Bill's first term as governor Hillary wasn't very involved in state politics. Now she began to take a more active role in his political life.

Hillary still didn't see why so many voters were

against her using the name Rodham. But she did see that her personal decision was going to cost her husband votes. At the beginning of the campaign Hillary made a surprise announcement: "From now on, I have decided to call myself Hillary Rodham Clinton." Insisting on being called by her maiden name, Rodham, wasn't worth the trouble it caused. "I gave it up," she said. "It just meant more to [the voters] than it did to me."

Hillary Rodham Clinton also made some changes in her wardrobe and hairstyle. Her long hair and casual clothes seemed to remind people in Arkansas that she was an outsider. So she cut her hair and started wearing suits and dresses. Since she and her husband represented the people, she would try to change her style to make them feel comfortable. Hillary wasn't the kind of person who paid attention to her appearance, although she was attractive. But she decided that she would try to fit in with the people of Arkansas so that they would give her their support. She felt it was a necessary step to take so that she could be effective in making more important changes.

One change that Hillary didn't mind making at all was getting rid of her thick glasses. She had always hated them, but she couldn't get used to wearing contact lenses. By this time, however, there were new types of contact lenses available. She was relieved to learn that she was able to use them.

Bill Clinton won the election in 1982, and the Clintons moved back into the governor's house. Now that Bill had been given a second chance, he was determined to concentrate on a few important goals.

One of them was improving the state's school system. Governor Clinton decided to appoint Hillary chairman of a committee on education reform.

Many people wondered if this was a good idea. Even Bill's own mother had her doubts. "Oh, my God, the man has lost his mind!" she thought. She knew Hillary could do a good job. But what if the voters didn't like the changes she made? They would blame the Clintons personally.

Hillary began traveling around the state, talking to parents, teachers, and students. There are seventy-five counties in Arkansas, and she visited every one of them. She found that many schools didn't have enough courses in math, science, and foreign languages. Even their best students couldn't get into many colleges. One of the things she told parents was that academics must rate at least as high as basketball. High school sports are important in Arkansas, as they are in many states. Hillary's message wasn't always easy for her audiences to accept.

Many of the changes her committee recommended turned out to be popular. Classes got smaller, and teachers' salaries were raised. But other changes were controversial. Many people didn't like the idea of merging small country schools into larger ones. One new policy that upset a lot of people was making all the teachers in the state take a test to prove they knew the subjects they were teaching. Many teachers who had been in the classroom for years felt insulted. On the day the test was given, some teachers came out with picket signs to protest the exam. Hillary called that day one of the worst of her life.

Some teachers never did forgive Hillary for making them take that test. But overall the educational reforms were popular. Even some of Mrs. Clinton's toughest critics thought she had done a good job.

Hillary's work on school reform also changed the way the people of Arkansas saw her. She had met and talked to thousands of people from all parts of the state. Now that they knew her better, they no longer thought of her as an outsider. One thing they learned was that she was not as different as they had imagined. Hillary was a religious person, who went to the Methodist church every Sunday. And although she was married to the governor, she did her own grocery shopping. She had even learned to cook southern foods, like the grits that Bill liked to eat for breakfast.

By 1984 Hillary Rodham Clinton had become a respected First Lady. That year the readers of the *Arkansas Times* voted her "Woman of the Year." She was invited to speak before groups all over the state.

In fact, national magazines were taking notice of the Clintons. *Esquire* magazine named them to a list of the most promising leaders of their generation.

But for all their success the Clintons also faced family problems in the mid-1980s. Roger Clinton, Bill's younger half-brother, had become involved with drugs. One day a representative of the state police came to the governor's office. He told Bill that Roger Clinton was suspected of selling drugs. What should they do?

"Handle it the way you would any other case," Bill told him.

Governor Clinton told Hillary that Roger was being

investigated. But the police had asked them not to tell anyone else in the family. It was a hard secret to keep but in the long run would help Roger. After a time Roger was arrested, forcing him to face his problem. The Clintons helped him find counseling to get off drugs.

In 1986 Governor Clinton was also facing his toughest reelection campaign since 1980. Once again his opponent was Frank White, the man who had criticized Hillary for calling herself Hillary Rodham. And for a second time White attacked the Clintons' personal life.

The Clintons tried to prepare Chelsea for the life of a politician's child. Chelsea was now six years old, and she knew that people on TV and in the newspapers were criticizing her parents. But she didn't understand why. To help her understand, Bill and Hillary staged mock debates while sitting around their kitchen table. Chelsea played the role of her father. Her parents would take turns pretending to be his opponent. "Bill Clinton has been a terrible governor," they would say. "He's no good at all."

At first Chelsea was on the verge of tears. Why would anyone say that about her daddy? But after a while she began to understand. It would never be easy for her to hear her parents being criticized by strangers. But it was something she would learn to get used to.

Bill Clinton won reelection that year. Almost immediately some friends and supporters tried to persuade him to run for president in 1988. He had dreamed of being president ever since high school, when he had visited the White House as part of the Boys' State delegation. But it would be very difficult for a governor from a small state to get elected to the White House. Running for president would turn his life upside down. And chances were good that it would all be for nothing.

And what about Hillary?

As a partner at the Rose Law Firm, Hillary was successful enough to be named one of the one hundred most powerful lawyers in the United States. She served on the boards of some major companies such as Wal-Mart, the discount-store chain. She continued to write articles about children's rights. And somehow she also found time to start a program that showed mothers how to prepare their young children to get the most out of school. As a presidential candidate's wife she would have almost no time for these projects. She had already taken time out of her career for motherhood and to help her husband in his races for governor. Now she would have to leave her work again.

But the Clintons' greatest concern was Chelsea. She had just gone through her father's campaign for governor. That was nothing compared to a presidential race. Candidates for president spend about a year and a half on the campaign trail. During that time both Bill and Hillary would have to do a lot of traveling. Chelsea would be left with a nanny for days at a time.

In July 1987 Governor Clinton called a news conference. Hundreds of reporters showed up. They were sure he was going to announce that he was running for president. But Bill Clinton surprised everyone. He told the press that he wouldn't be a candidate after all. He said that Chelsea was the main reason for the decision. He and Hillary were afraid that a campaign might be too hard on her. "Our daughter is seven. She is the most important person in the world to us, and our most important responsibility."

The decision gave Chelsea four more years out of the national spotlight and four more years to grow in her close-knit family. She played softball on a team called the Molar Rollers, sponsored by a local dentist. She took ballet lessons. When she performed in dance recitals, Chelsea was embarrassed by her dad because he would wave at her from his seat in the audience and try to get her to smile.

On Sundays, Hillary Rodham Clinton still attended the Methodist church. Bill was a Baptist. Chelsea was allowed to choose which church to attend. She eventually decided to join her mother's church.

Chelsea was also allowed to choose her own clothes. But in other ways the Clintons were fairly strict. They believed their responsibility as parents was to give loving but firm discipline. They limited the number of hours Chelsea could watch TV and wouldn't let her see some movies that her friends were going to.

One ongoing family argument was on the subject of pierced ears. Some of Chelsea's girlfriends had them, but the Clintons didn't like the idea. They warned Chelsea that her ears could get infected and enlisted both her grandmothers to try to talk her out of it. Chelsea listened to all their arguments and decided that she still wanted pierced ears. Finally her parents told her she could go ahead—but she would have to wait until she turned thirteen.

But in 1991 the Clintons faced a decision that was a lot more difficult than whether Chelsea should get her ears pierced. Another round of presidential primaries was coming up. Would Governor Clinton get into the race this time? The Clintons and their friends spent many hours debating what to do.

In the meantime some people were suggesting that Hillary run for Congress. Others thought she ought to run for governor, taking over from Bill if he became a presidential candidate. Hillary said that she loved public service, but she didn't enjoy being in the spotlight all the time. "Since I was in eighth grade, people have been urging me to run for office," Hillary said later. "But it just wasn't anything I was interested in."

Unlike Hillary, Bill Clinton really enjoyed campaigning. He loved meeting new people. He never seemed to get tired of answering questions. For Hillary it was often a chore. She didn't mind giving speeches or interviews. But four or five speeches in a single day—and even more interviews—was a challenge. Yet in recent times the wives of political candidates often do almost as much campaigning as their husbands. Hillary would have to go on the campaign trail whether she enjoyed it or not.

For Chelsea's part, she was eleven and better able to handle a tough campaign. And now all three of her grandparents were nearby. Hugh Rodham was retired, and he and Dorothy had moved to Little Rock.

They lived not far from the Clintons, and they could look after Chelsea when her parents were away.

The Clintons discussed the idea of Bill's candidacy with each other. They also talked about it with friends. Often the discussions were held around a table in the kitchen in the governor's house.

In late summer 1991, the Clintons made their decision. This time they were ready. Bill Clinton was going to run for president of the United States.

The Race

"Running for president is like pitching a no-hitter," Hillary Rodham Clinton said shortly after Bill announced that he would be a candidate. A pitcher has to concentrate on one batter at a time. If he starts to think about his chances of getting through the game without giving up a hit, he'll be too nervous to pitch well.

At the beginning of the 1992 campaign, the odds that Bill Clinton would become president were even smaller than that of an average pitcher having a no-hitter. There were seven candidates competing for the Democratic party's nomination for president. Reporters jokingly called the Democratic candidates "the seven dwarfs." And even if Bill beat them all in the primaries, almost everyone agreed that no Democrat had much of a chance of defeating President Bush in the general election. George Bush was so popular that it seemed he would win easily.

Even though the odds were against them, the Clintons went to work. Both Bill and Hillary spent a lot of time traveling in other states. Hillary almost always went to different cities than her husband. Usually she had one other person with her, the woman who served as her press secretary.

71

Hillary tried not to be away from home more than three or four days at a time. And like most working mothers who travel, she spent much of her free time on the phone with her daughter. After a long day of rushing from one appointment to the next, she would go back to her hotel room and call home so that she could help Chelsea with her homework. Often Chelsea would fax her assignments to her mother's hotel so that they could go over the work together.

Bill Clinton did well in the early primaries. But success brought problems. News reporters as well as the other candidates made targets of the Clintons. A lot of the criticism was aimed at Hillary. Some people weren't sure they wanted a First Lady who had strong opinions on the issues. Some weren't even sure they wanted a First Lady who was smart. Former President Richard Nixon put it bluntly: "If the wife comes through as being too strong and too intelligent, it makes the husband look like a wimp."

Bill Clinton laughed off these attacks. "I've always liked strong women," he said. "It doesn't bother me for people to see her and get excited and say she could be president too."

Other critics were uncomfortable about Hillary's career in law. Jerry Brown, who was running against Bill Clinton in the primaries, wondered aloud if Hillary's law firm got special treatment because she was the governor's wife. Hillary was in Chicago when some reporters met her on the street and told her about Brown's question. Hillary explained to reporters that she never took a share of the money when her firm did business with the state.

But the questions about her career kept coming up. Hillary began to wonder why she should apologize for being a successful lawyer. "I suppose I could have just stayed home and baked cookies and had teas," she said during one interview. Hillary went on to say that she thought women had the right to choose between staying home and having a full- or part-time career. But these remarks didn't make it to the evening news. It sounded as if Hillary had a low opinion of homemakers.

Were a lot of women offended by Hillary Rodham Clinton's thoughts on cookie baking? It's hard to say. But the people who write editorials thought so. They complained that Hillary felt superior to women who didn't have careers outside the home. Hillary herself said the reaction to her statement taught her how important it is to communicate clearly.

In the meantime other reporters looked up the articles that Hillary had written over the years about children's rights. Hillary had always been a strong supporter of children. She wrote about such things as giving children a way to legally get out of abusive home lives. She believed that teenagers should be treated with respect, and that they had a right to make important decisions in their lives. One of her articles stated that under some circumstances children should have the right to sue their parents. If the Clintons were elected, some Republicans charged, any kid who thought his parents were too strict would be able to take them to court!

Mrs. Clinton explained that this just wasn't true. "I'm talking about the rights of children in extreme cases, such as abuse." In these cases children sometimes might have to go to court to win the right to be adopted by their foster parents.

In the same conversation with an Arkansas acquaintance, she went on to explain her goals. "What I am is probably so corny that people just don't want to believe it. I'm interested in . . . public service."

In fact, the real argument between Hillary Rodham Clinton and her critics probably had to do with their different ideas of public service. Hillary wanted the government to try to provide for the needs of families and children. Republicans, and even some Democrats, wondered if there weren't limits to what the government could do. They argued that government programs aimed at solving social problems cost a lot of money and often didn't work anyway.

The role of government is a complicated issue. But in presidential campaigns sometimes the issues get forgotten. If an alien from outer space had landed on Earth in 1992, he might well have thought that the American election was about cookies! One magazine managed to get recipes for chocolate chip cookies from both Hillary and the then-present First Lady, Barbara Bush. It asked its readers to choose which was the best. A bakery in Washington, D.C., got into the spirit and delivered thousands of cookies to Washington restaurants. Customers were invited to conduct their own taste tests.

Even *Consumer Reports* did a cookie comparison. Their testers liked Barbara Bush's cookies, but they liked Hillary's even better. In fact, Hillary's recipe won out over two of the most popular brands of chocolate chip cookies in the country, Mrs. Fields and Famous Amos.

The visitor from outer space might also have thought that the election was about Hillary's looks. Radio commentators made fun of Hillary's hairdos and the headbands she liked to wear.

People saw Hillary Rodham Clinton as a symbol of all kinds of issues. Sometimes she felt that people's opinions had nothing to do with who she was or what she said. She just happened to be handy. She confessed that she kept thinking of the nursery rhyme that goes:

As I was standing in the street as quiet as can be
A great big ugly man came up and tied his horse to me.

In May 1992 Hillary was invited to give a speech at the Wellesley College commencement ceremonies. It was twenty-three years since she had spoken there at her own graduation. In her talk she tried to explain her feelings about the tough choices that young women have to make: Women who don't get married are considered "abnormal." Women who marry but don't have children are considered "selfish yuppies." Women who stay home to take care of their children are told, "You've wasted your education." Yet women who work outside the home are criticized for being bad mothers.

"So you see," she concluded, "if you listen to all those people who make those rules you might conclude that the safest course of action is just to take your diploma and crawl under your bed."

The people in the audience burst out laughing.

But Hillary hadn't finished. "Hold on to your dreams, whatever they are," she told the graduates. "Care about something you needn't bother with at all. Throw yourself into the world and make your voice count."

As Hillary traveled around the country, she often spoke in schools. Often these school visits were the highlights of her week. She even went back to Maine South High, the school she attended in the 1960s. But in many schools she noticed one thing that bothered her. Sometimes when she finished a speech and asked for questions, only boys raised their hands. The girls were quiet. They reminded her of her own friends in junior high and high school.

"I'd like to see a girl's hand," Hillary would say whenever that happened.

At one school Hillary talked about the problem of girls staying quietly in the background. For many of them getting interested in boys meant losing interest in schoolwork. She remembered feeling these pressures when she was a teenager. Now she was thankful that she hadn't let the pressures discourage her from doing well in her classes.

That June, not long after Hillary's speech at Wellesley, the Clintons headed to California. It would be their final campaign effort before that state's primary election. In Los Angeles they stayed at the home of the Clintons' Arkansas friends Linda Bloodworth-Thomason and her husband, the producers of the TV show *Evening Shade*. On the afternoon of primary day, when their campaigning was over, Hillary was invited to the house of actress Markie Post to watch a tape of a new show the actress was going to star in.

Instead the house party turned out to be a Hillary makeover. A hairstylist cut her hair and lightened it. A makeup expert showed her how to use eye shadow and blush to make her face look softer. Representatives of several stores also showed up with samples of clothes. As Hillary tried on the outfits a professional wardrobe consultant advised her on which looked best. Hillary chose a new wardrobe of suits, mostly in light pastel shades.

That day the California voters went for Bill Clinton. At the victory party that night the public got its first look at Hillary's new image.

Makeovers can be fun—even if it isn't fun to be told that you might need one. Some of Hillary's old friends weren't happy with the changes they saw. They believed that not only was Hillary's wardrobe changing but her behavior was becoming different too. Although she still made campaign speeches, she was very careful about what she said. Her friends feared that she was starting to look more and more like a TV personality, not an ordinary person. One Arkansas man who had known Hillary for years complained that his bright, outspoken friend was being turned into a kind of "robot." Hillary insisted that she didn't feel that way. She didn't mind improving herself, especially if it would help her husband win the election. But it must have been hard for her to have to realize that the public put so much importance on her looks.

One thing that did upset Hillary more deeply was the discovery that many voters didn't know she had a daughter. The Clintons had tried very hard to give Chelsea a normal childhood. They didn't bring her along on the campaign trail, and they kept her away from reporters and photographers. Hillary thought this was what good parents should do. But the result was that people didn't realize she was a mother at all! The Clintons finally decided to let *People* magazine run a feature on Chelsea. And she would soon begin to attend some political events. Allowing a spotlight on Chelsea bothered Hillary more than the changes she had to make in her own clothes and campaigning style.

Still, by the time Hillary arrived at the Democratic convention in July, she did seem to be enjoying herself more. Because Bill had won the California primary, everyone knew that he would be the Democratic nominee.

TV cameras followed Bill, Hillary, and Chelsea as they walked hand in hand from their New York City hotel to Madison Square Garden. There cheering delegates were waiting to welcome Bill Clinton as the official candidate of the Democratic party. On the podium Hillary looked proud and happy. The Clintons had worked hard for this moment. But even harder work lay ahead. Now presidential candidate Bill Clinton would have to persuade even more Americans to vote for the Democratic ticket.

In late spring, during the primary campaign, Bill Clinton had asked Al Gore to be his running mate. Gore, who was also from the South, accepted and became the vice-presidential nominee. Hillary got along well with Senator Gore and Tipper Gore, his wife. During the election campaign the Clintons and the Gores toured the country by bus. Often their campaign bus was on the road from six A.M. to well after midnight. The Clintons and the Gores shook thousands and thousands of hands. Somehow they managed to get by on a few hours of sleep a night and still look cheerful.

In the meantime the Republicans were having some problems. The theme of the Republican convention was family values, but sometimes the message got confused. It looked as though their speakers were attacking Hillary just because she was a married woman who had a career.

In the long run the personal attacks on Hillary probably backfired. It was hard for many Americans to see just how Hillary Rodham Clinton was different from the Republican vice president's wife, Marilyn Quayle. After all, Mrs. Quayle had a law degree too and was a confident, outspoken campaigner.

After months of almost nonstop campaigning, Election Day came at last. On November 3, 1992, the Clintons and the Gores were in Little Rock, awaiting the election results. Early in the evening it became apparent that they had won. They had beaten Republican president George Bush and the independent candidate, Ross Perot. The victorious candidates and their wives went outside to greet the huge crowd that had gathered to applaud them. The jubilant Clintons waved to old friends in the crowd. Then the newly elected president and Hillary danced to the campaign's unofficial theme song, Fleetwood Mac's "Don't Stop Thinking About Tomorrow." President-elect Bill Clinton and soon-to-be First Lady Hillary Rodham Clinton would now have to be doing a lot of thinking about their tomorrows.

At Home in the White House

On January 20, 1993, William Jefferson Clinton was sworn in as president of the United States. Hillary Rodham Clinton was beside him, holding a family Bible that he used to take the oath of office. For America it was the day to celebrate the change-over from one president's administration to that of another. But for the Clintons it was also moving day.

In one way moving was easier for the Clintons than for the average family. When you are the new residents of the White House, you don't have to worry about unpacking boxes. On the morning of Inauguration Day, while the various ceremonies were going on, a team of movers was hard at work in the White House. The last of the Bushes' belongings were whisked away, and the Clintons' possessions were set in place. Even their clothes were unpacked.

For Chelsea the inauguration was an adventure. The arrival of a new president in Washington is celebrated with formal parties, called inaugural balls. One of the parties was being sponsored by MTV, the rock-music network on cable TV. Twelve-year-old Chelsea was given permission to attend it. During the afternoon she and her girlfriends raced around the private quarters of the White House, comparing their new dresses, working on their hairdos, and talking about the evening to come.

The ball was fun. But the next day the Clintons had to get up early for still more festivities. That afternoon they arrived home tired and hungry. The new president joked that this would be a good time to order a pizza. He pretended to be upset when he learned that it would be impossible. The Secret Service doesn't like delivery boys wandering around the White House.

Although the Clintons didn't mind doing without their pizza, they soon found out that getting used to living in the White House would be a challenge for all of them. Even Socks, Chelsea's pet cat, would have to adjust. The first time Socks ventured outside to sniff around the grounds of his new home, he was surrounded by photographers. A few of them even got down on the ground and crawled toward him to get close-up photographs. Socks looked startled, if not offended, and hurried back inside.

Although the White House is the president's home, it is also a public building. Its West Wing is filled with offices. Every year thousands of tourists line up for a chance to see the beautiful and historic rooms, where state dinners and receptions are held. Even the private rooms upstairs, where the First Family lives, are filled with reminders of the building's great history. One bedroom has the same bed that Abraham Lincoln slept in 130 years ago!

Hillary had been preparing for her new life in the

White House almost since the election was over. She had her first look at the Clintons' new residence when Barbara Bush invited her to tea. Even though the election campaign seemed to pit the two of them against each other, they got along well when they met for tea. Mrs. Bush was very helpful in giving the incoming First Lady advice on how to survive in a house that leaves very little room for privacy.

Hillary also prepared for her new role as First Lady by reading books—forty-three books in all—about the history of the White House and the lives of former First Ladies.

One thing she learned in her reading was that she was not really the first president's wife to have held a paying job. A number of other First Ladies worked, though usually before they were married. Jacqueline Kennedy had been a newspaper photographer, and Betty Ford had performed with a modern-dance troupe. Eleanor Roosevelt wrote a newspaper column while her husband was in the White House.

Hillary Rodham Clinton must also have learned that no one is really sure what the First Lady's role should be. The men who wrote the Constitution of the United States didn't mention the First Lady. It didn't even occur to them that being the president's wife might be a job at all. But Martha Washington was the first to find out otherwise. She complained that she was expected to play hostess to hundreds of strangers. She received so many guests that they wore out the furniture in a few months!

Two hundred years after Martha Washington, the president's furniture still gets worn out very quickly.

Even in the private rooms there is a lot of traffic. Secret Service agents and aides to the president are constantly coming and going. Then there are the times that TV crews get invited for an interview, bringing with them bright lights and heavy sound equipment. So much activity takes its toll on the White House.

Like previous First Families, the Clintons did some renovating, using money raised by their friends. It was up to Hillary to decide what changes to make. One room that she didn't feel comfortable with was the family's dining room. At the governor's residence in Arkansas, the Clintons often ate in the kitchen. Hillary had the family's old table and some wicker chairs they used in Little Rock shipped to the White House. Then she discovered that the room occupied by Secret Service agents who are on duty guarding the president was near Chelsea's room. She moved the Secret Service men farther away so that Chelsea could have more privacy.

Hillary also found herself taking on other traditional tasks of the First Lady. She had to pick the colors for the tablecloths and napkins at state dinners and approve the menus. One change she made was that smoking is no longer allowed in the White House.

The Clintons soon found that some things about living in the White House are a lot of fun. There is a bowling alley in the basement and a small screening room for watching movies. The president's family doesn't have to wait for movies to come out on video. Just as in a regular movie theater, they can get prints of new films right at home. Movie night at the Clinton

White House is usually Friday. Among the films the First Family saw during the early part of 1993 were *Groundhog Day* and *Aladdin.*

Hillary especially liked *Dave,* a comedy about a man who looks just like the president. In the movie the president becomes ill and a look-alike takes his place. "I thought it was a really fun movie. But I know now that I could never keep a secret like that," she joked.

Soon after moving into her famous new address, Hillary said that what she missed most from her old life wasn't privacy but "mobility." She's not free to move about as she wishes. She can't just pull on a jogging suit and go for a long walk. Her Secret Service guards need to know in advance where she is going, and they have to go with her. And because Hillary has become famous, everyone recognizes her. Wherever she goes, there are people who want to see her and even speak to her. Photographers pop up everywhere, and often her picture appears in the next day's paper, sometimes with comments about her outfit and hairdo.

Even at home the First Lady had to get used to a whole new way of living. She had to learn how to deal with the White House staff, who are called stewards. One day soon after the inauguration Chelsea become ill with a virus. Late that night she woke up hungry and asked her mother to fix her some scrambled eggs. As soon as Hillary went to the kitchen and started looking for a frying pan, a steward appeared. He explained that it was his job to cook the eggs. Hillary had to do some fast talking. She explained that she would rather do the cooking herself. She knew exactly how Chelsea liked her scrambled eggs. The steward went away, but she wasn't sure if she had hurt his feelings or not. After trying so hard during the presidential campaign to convince voters that she really did know how to cook, now Hillary discovered that as First Lady she was supposed to stay out of the kitchen.

Of course, most of the time the White House stewards make a First Family's life run very smoothly. For one thing, the First Lady doesn't have to do housework. At first Hillary did try to do a few chores just to keep in touch with the way normal people live. But she soon found out that even simple tasks were now complicated.

Stocking a new kitchen was one example. Every family has its favorite foods. When it came time to stock the Clintons' private kitchen, Hillary sat down to make out a shopping list for the stewards. Trying to remember the right brands, sizes, and varieties was taking a lot of time. She decided that it would be easier to make the first shopping trip herself. Then the staff could just replace items as they were used up.

One day that week Hillary picked up Chelsea after school. Their driver took them to a local supermarket, where they loaded up the cart with cereal, peanut butter, and other foods the Clintons like. When they got to the checkout counter, Hillary opened her wallet. She was embarrassed to see that she had only eleven dollars. Because of working on the campaign and election, it had been a long time since Hillary had done her own shopping. She'd forgotten to check to see how much money she had before she left home!

Of course, by then everyone in the store was watching the famous customers. The manager went over to the checkout counter to make sure the First Lady got good service.

"Do you take credit cards?" the president's wife asked.

The manager gulped. He was even more embarrassed than the First Lady. "We're going to start next month."

Hillary could have asked to charge her groceries. But that would only have put the manager on the spot. The next day he might have other customers demanding equal treatment! "That means I can't buy all this now," Hillary concluded. She and Chelsea picked out a few items she could pay for and left the rest of the groceries behind.

Although there were a few awkward incidents like this one, for the most part Hillary Rodham Clinton adjusted easily to the First Lady's role. Her years as the First Lady of Arkansas and on the campaign trail were good preparation. She had gotten used to being photographed everywhere she went and to attending many official receptions.

Chelsea Clinton had a bigger adjustment to make. In Arkansas, Chelsea had been the governor's daughter, but her friends had grown used to that. It no longer impressed them very much. In Washington, as the daughter of the United States president, Chelsea's life would be very different.

Chelsea

In January 1993 Hillary Rodham and Bill Clinton made an announcement: Chelsea Clinton would be attending a private school called Sidwell Friends.

Sidwell is one of the oldest private schools in Washington. The students' parents must pay to send them there. Many stories were printed in the newspapers once the Clintons' decision to send Chelsea to Sidwell was made. Some people were upset by this. They thought Chelsea should go to a public school, like most American children.

But it was hard to see how the president's daughter could fit in at a big public high school. For one thing, there would be Secret Service agents in the building every day. If Chelsea missed school to travel with her parents, she might need special assignments. The school would give Chelsea more privacy than a public school. Hillary decided this would be best for her daughter. One of the First Lady's main concerns was that Chelsea be given as "normal" a life as possible. So in the end her parents had chosen a school that was used to having students from famous families.

In the early 1900s Archy Roosevelt, the son of President Theodore Roosevelt, went to Sidwell. Over the years many other famous people have been enrolled there. Today many Sidwell students have parents who work for newspapers or TV stations. Parents of others have jobs in government. They are used to meeting famous people.

The news that Chelsea Clinton was going to Sidwell caught the students by surprise. To get them ready, the teachers held special discussion groups.

Students were asked to pretend they were Chelsea trying to make friends. "How would you feel in her place?" the teachers asked.

The school principal asked students not to talk about Chelsea to reporters. There were other rules too. Classroom doors would be kept locked. If a student got to class late, he or she was supposed to knock and ask permission to be let in.

Some of the kids wondered if they would have to remember passwords and use them to prove to the Secret Service that they belonged on the school grounds. "We thought the world was ending because our freedom was being taken away," one student said. "We were mad about that."

The students' feelings were just one more reason for Chelsea to feel nervous about starting school. Chelsea was due to join the eighth grade at Sidwell on January 25, a few days after the inauguration. That morning her mother picked out a cute pants outfit for her to wear. When Chelsea saw it, she made a face. "Oh, Mom," she said, "no one will be wearing anything *like* that." Instead she put on a sweatshirt and jeans.

Hillary had decided to drive Chelsea to school that morning. Having your mother take you to school the first day might not be ideal, but it was a lot better than going in a limousine with Secret Service men for company. Bodyguards were watching the Clintons, but they did their best to stay in the background.

When they reached Sidwell, reporters and photographers were camped out on the steps. Hillary drove Chelsea to a back entrance. She had time to notice that Chelsea's choice of wardrobe had been the right one. The other girls were wearing jeans too.

Before long the Sidwell students decided that having the president's daughter in class wasn't so bad after all. After a while some of the rules about locked doors were relaxed. "Once she got on campus," a student said, "we realized that she was just a kid like the rest of us."

When Sidwell Friends had its winter carnival, Chelsea was one of two girls who volunteered to dress up as fortune-tellers. She sat in a booth and the students came one by one to have their palms read. No one took the fortunes seriously. But Chelsea was good at making up things to say.

The boy who had been so upset about her coming to the school was one of her customers. After getting his fortune told, he decided that Chelsea was a thoughtful person. When she realized that more people were lining up for her booth, she took a break so that the other girl telling fortunes wouldn't feel left out.

The boy also thought that Chelsea had a good sense of humor. Later he remembered some of the things Chelsea had told one of his classmates: "You have a very strange hand. . . . You will marry at forty-five and have a couple of kids. You'll have a great sex life."

"Thank you," said the classmate.

On most days Chelsea Clinton's routine wasn't very different from that of other students at Sidwell. She liked math and was very good at it. In the winter she played on the school soccer team. Sometimes her mother showed up to watch the games. In the spring she played softball. Chelsea started taking ballet lessons again and visiting the homes of friends.

In the White House, Chelsea does homework and talks to friends on the phone. When President Clinton has time, he likes to play cards with his daughter. Chelsea also plays video games. One day when she was home sick from school, she taught her mother how to play Game Boy. Now Mrs. Clinton sometimes takes Game Boy along as a way to relax when she is traveling.

On her thirteenth birthday, February 27, Chelsea was allowed to have some of her friends sleep over at the White House. She invited some girls she went to school with in Little Rock and new friends from Sidwell Friends.

Chelsea's life is probably about as normal as it can be for a teenager living in the White House. Still, people are always curious about the children of presidents. This is nothing new. Even back in 1904 the newspapers wrote about the pranks young Archy Roosevelt played. (One story was that he smuggled his pony upstairs in the White House elevator and hid it in his bedroom!)

91

One day during the spring of 1993 Chelsea and her father went to a bookstore together, and they were quickly surrounded by photographers. The names of the books they bought were printed in the newspapers.

Even Chelsea's arguments with her parents aren't really private: In June, when Hillary Rodham Clinton was interviewed on national television, one of the first things reporter Katie Couric asked was when Chelsea would be allowed to get her ears pierced. Then Couric added, "These days she'll probably want to pierce her nose."

"Oh, please!" Mrs. Clinton protested. "That's one of those things that Bill and I say, 'After you're twenty-one and on your own and out of the house, but not before.'"

One weekend soon after the election *Saturday Night Live* did a sketch making fun of Chelsea's braces and hair. This time Hillary came to her daughter's defense. Hillary had nothing against *Saturday Night Live*. She laughed when the same show did a skit about her. She just thought it wasn't fair to pick on a teenager. She wondered whether the show's producer "had nothing better to do than to be mean and cruel to a young girl." After hearing her complaints, the producer decided not to do any more Chelsea jokes.

"When I was growing up, my parents taught me to do what was right and not listen to other people," Hillary recalled when asked about the *Saturday Night Live* skit featuring Chelsea. Still, no matter what advice teenagers get from their parents, they all want to be popular. Being singled out, even for good things like getting high grades, can be uncomfortable. Hillary had been singled out that way when she was in school. "That was hard for me," she said, "and I didn't have one millionth of the attention she'll have."

Like her mother, Chelsea sometimes thought about becoming an astronaut. Now women are accepted into the astronaut program, so it's not an impossible dream. In the summer of 1993 Chelsea attended the United States Space Camp in Huntsville, Alabama. For five days she and her fellow campers learned about the life of an astronaut. They built and launched model rockets. Then they divided into groups for simulated shuttle missions that were set up just like a real trip in the shuttle. Chelsea's group won a prize for being the best team.

One thing Chelsea doesn't want to be when she grows up is a politician. She once said that she gets tired of hearing so much talk about politics. At least that's the way she feels now.

Hillary Rodham Clinton has faith that whatever Chelsea decides to do in the future, she would be able to handle the pressure of being famous. "I think the world would be a better place if more people were to define themselves in terms of their own standards and values and not what other people said or thought about them. It's tough when you are an adolescent, because peer opinion and other people's opinion become more important. But I think she'll be okay."

Not Just the Boss's Wife

With her family settled in at the White House and Chelsea in school, Hillary had more time to spend on another of the roles she would fill—helping the president develop new policies.

After the November election a lot of people wondered whether Hillary would be active in the government during the next four years. Would she be her husband's partner, a sort of co-president? Would she be his chief of staff? Or would she take on a "safe" role, like working for better schools, and work behind the scenes?

Four days after the inauguration President Clinton surprised almost everyone by announcing that he had asked Hillary to serve as the head of the task force on health care.

At the time Bill Clinton took office, about 37 million Americans had no insurance that would pay their medical bills. Some of these people were unemployed. Some worked for companies that didn't have insurance plans for their employees. Sometimes insurance companies refused to take on people who had serious illnesses. The task force that Hillary headed would recommend new laws to make sure all the people who had been left out for one reason or another were covered by insurance. It would also look into ways to control the rising costs of medical care.

Hillary Rodham Clinton's new job was an important position that could change the lives of all Americans. And it would place her in the middle of a long and heated national debate. Since the 1950s politicians have been debating ways to make the health-care system more fair. Health care is an issue with many sides to it, and almost everyone has strong opinions about it. Many people agree that it is wrong that some very ill people cannot get insurance. But good medical care is expensive, and it gets more expensive every year. Doctors and scientists keep discovering new drugs and treatments. How much treatment does everyone have a right to receive? And who will pay for it?

Most people have their own doctors, whom they feel comfortable with. They worry that if the system changes, they won't be able to see the doctors they like. And the doctors themselves worry that an insurance company or the government will tell them how to take care of their patients.

Many people wondered if Bill Clinton hadn't made a big mistake in asking his wife to take over the difficult job of heading the health-care task force. If its conclusions were unpopular, what would the president do? Could he fire his own wife? Even some women who admired Hillary thought she was foolish to take on this assignment. Why would she want to be just "the boss's wife" when she could have a job of her own outside the government?

President Clinton knew about these questions, but he still thought his wife was the right person for the job. After all, many people in Arkansas had warned of trouble when Hillary took on education reform in that state. Yet the project had worked out well in the end.

The health-care task force was a long-term project. Hillary Rodham Clinton started traveling around the country, talking to doctors, health-care workers, and average people. She and her staff listened to advice from hundreds of experts. Then they began to think about specific proposals. In the end they came up with a report that was over a thousand pages long.

In the meantime many people suspected that Hillary was also giving her husband advice on matters other than health care, such as whom to appoint for government jobs. *Time* magazine even called Mrs. Clinton "the most powerful First Lady in history."

This was probably true. But just how does Hillary's role differ from that of former First Ladies?

The fact is that many presidents have relied on their wives for political advice. Everyone knows this happens, yet people don't like to hear about it. After all, they voted for the president, not the First Lady. They would just as soon have the First Lady be in the background. The first president's wife to be criticized for getting too involved in politics was Abigail Adams, who was married to our second president, John Adams. Mrs. Adams's critics said she helped her husband pick federal judges.

In Abigail Adams's time most Americans thought that women had no place in public life. They wanted the First Lady to be nothing more than a hostess.

Through time much more came to be expected of a First Lady, and Americans now place many demands on her.

Eleanor Roosevelt was very active in politics while her husband, Franklin Delano Roosevelt, was president. And since Jacqueline Kennedy was First Lady in the early 1960s, all presidents' wives have worked for good causes. In the mid-1960s, Lady Bird Johnson started a campaign to clean up highways and public places. In the late 1970s, Rosalynn Carter worked for the rights of women, the elderly, and the mentally ill. In the 1980s, Nancy Reagan urged young people to "just say no" to drugs. Barbara Bush, during her husband's term, raised money for literacy programs.

Strangely enough, the more these First Ladies tried to live up to what people expected of them, the more they were criticized:

Rosalynn Carter, the wife of President Jimmy Carter, sat in on a meeting of her husband's cabinet, the heads of the major government departments. Mrs. Carter was just trying to keep informed, but she was accused of pushing herself in where she didn't belong.

Nancy Reagan was criticized because she paid a lot of attention to the way she dressed. A few years later some people complained that Barbara Bush didn't dress up enough.

None of the First Ladies has ever gotten paid for her efforts. Neither does Hillary Rodham Clinton. In fact, a federal law prohibits the president from giving paying jobs to his wife or other close relatives.

In certain ways Hillary Rodham Clinton is different

from former First Ladies. Other First Ladies had offices in the East Wing of the White House. But Hillary set up her office in the West Wing, the area where the serious business of government is done. She also has more assistants and a larger staff than other First Ladies. About five hundred people worked for the health-care task force in one way or another.

The most important difference between Hillary Rodham Clinton and former First Ladies is that she has helped make official policy. She has even had to defend her ideas to members of Congress who have the power to approve, make compromises with or reject the ideas altogether. But if this has given Hillary Rodham Clinton more power than other presidents' wives ever had, she has been careful not to say so. Talking to the public about health care, Hillary presented herself as a concerned citizen and a mother, someone who was mainly gathering facts for the president.

In interviews Mrs. Clinton was careful to say that she took on the job because "Bill Clinton asked me to." In this way she showed that she understands the divided feelings Americans have about the role of the First Lady.

During the first few months after the inauguration it seemed that Hillary Rodham Clinton's greatest challenge in juggling her several roles would be finding time for herself. She would get up at six or six-thirty in the morning so that she could answer letters before going to her West Wing office. One day Hillary took part in thirty meetings—and this wasn't considered an especially busy day!

Although the president managed to go jogging in the mornings, exercise was one of the things Hillary did without.

"I need to get a good night's sleep once in a while," the First Lady told one interviewer who asked what she did in her spare time. "I feel like I'm a million hours behind some days, but I'm catching up."

People who work in the White House soon found that Hillary is very efficient. She is a hard worker who has no patience with staff members who waste time. But Hillary can also be fun to work for. The First Lady likes to lip-synch to old rock-and-roll songs. And she can do hilarious imitations, though she limits herself to imitating famous people who wouldn't be offended.

Hillary also has tried to look out for young, single staff members, urging them to take time off once in a while to enjoy life. "We're trying to get dates for them," she once laughingly told a reporter. "We are looking for dates."

When Hillary Rodham Clinton looked at her schedule in the spring of 1993, one event she looked forward to was the opening game of the season for the Chicago Cubs baseball team. When she was a girl, her father had often taken her to Cubs baseball games at Wrigley Field. Now she had been asked to throw out the first ball of the season at the same stadium.

Most important, Hugh Rodham would be there too. Hillary's father hadn't been well for a few years. He was in a wheelchair now. This was to be a very special day for him.

Less than three weeks before the opening day ceremony, Hillary was having lunch in the White House cafeteria when a member of her staff brought bad news. Hugh Rodham had suffered a stroke. Hillary and Chelsea flew home to Arkansas immediately. "When we got there, for the first couple of days he knew we were there, and it was wonderful," she said. But it was soon clear that Hugh Rodham would not recover.

Hillary stayed with her father for sixteen days. Of course, she didn't attend the baseball game. But there were some official duties she couldn't postpone. She wasn't able to be with her father when he died on April 7, 1993.

After Hugh Rodham's funeral Hillary's mother came to Washington to spend some time at the White House. Hillary Rodham Clinton now had a new role to add to all her others, that of a daughter trying to comfort her grieving parent.

Hillary herself drew strength from her religious faith. She also talked more about the need for balance between her work and home life. "What power wouldn't I trade for a little more time with my family?" she asked in one speech.

In the past it often seemed that the Clintons had trouble relaxing. Even when they were with friends, they thought and talked about work. But that summer of 1993 they took a real family vacation on the resort island of Martha's Vineyard off the coast of Massachusetts. Reporters who checked the president's schedule were surprised to see that it listed no appointments. The plan for one day was "Vegging out." Hillary got to catch up on some of the sleep she had missed. But there were outings too. Hillary and Chelsea went souvenir shopping, and the Clintons were invited to go sailing with Senator Edward Kennedy and Jacqueline Kennedy Onassis, who summer on the island.

When the health-care task force was formed, it was supposed to finish its work in one hundred days. For several reasons, including the time Hillary took off during her father's illness, the job took a few months longer. But by late September 1993 its report was ready.

Along the way an unexpected thing happened. Some of the same people who had been Hillary's critics in the past became fans of hers. She had proved to these people that she had great skills in organizing, researching, and analyzing and in working with others. Even Senator Robert Dole, the leader of the Senate's Republicans, said that Hillary was someone he looked forward to working with.

The press too had kind words for Hillary Rodham Clinton. A reporter on public television observed that Hillary was a success because, unlike many people in politics, "she speaks in plain English."

When the moment came to announce the specifics of the health-care plan, President Clinton, not his wife, was in the spotlight. On September 22, 1993, he made a major speech to Congress. As President Clinton stood before the senators and representatives, television cameras from all the networks were trained on him. Hillary was seated in the balcony, along with all the other spectators. But the first time her name was mentioned, the members of Congress rose in a standing ovation. Hillary stood briefly, then quickly sat down.

The applause continued for several minutes. Tipper Gore, the vice president's wife, had to urge Hillary to stand up again and acknowledge the ovation. Hillary looked a little uneasy, as if she was worried about being accused of stealing the spotlight from her husband. But she also looked proud.

Two days later the ABC evening news program named Hillary its "Person of the Week." Hillary Rodham Clinton, the report said, had proved that a First Lady could perform valuable service for the nation. She was "not just the boss's wife."

Hillary Goes to the Hill

The week after the president's announcement on the new health-care proposals, Hillary Rodham Clinton appeared at the Capitol building; on Capitol Hill, where the Senate and the House of Representatives meet. She would be testifying before the House Ways and Means Committee and the Senate Finance Committee. The committee members would ask her to explain the health plan and how much it would cost.

These two congressional committees are among the toughest audiences in the world. Many witnesses who come before them bring stacks of papers and whole teams of aides and lawyers to back them up. Hillary showed up alone, and smiling.

Without using notes she answered all the questions the committee members put to her. Not only did she know a great deal about health care but she had studied the committee members themselves and knew how to appeal to them as individuals. When one of them asked her about the price of prescription drugs, she showed by her answer that she knew he was a pharmacist in private life.

Not all the committee members were sure they liked the health plan. But they did like Hillary Rodham

Clinton. At the end of the session they gave her another standing ovation. The debate over health care was just beginning. But Hillary Rodham Clinton had shown that a president's wife could take the challenge of such a huge job.

In the long run Hillary Rodham Clinton's ability to serve as a role model for working women may be as important as her work on health-care reform. This is obvious from the mail she received.

All the Clintons get a lot of mail. Even Socks, humorously referred to as the First Cat, gets bags of it. In the first part of 1993 the First Family received about seventy thousand letters every month, many more than President and Mrs. Bush got. This often had nothing to do with politics. Many people who wrote disagreed with President Clinton's programs. But the letter writers seemed to feel close to the Clintons, as if they knew them personally. "They just write 'Dear Bill and Hillary,'" said the woman in charge of the White House mail. The writers all treat the Clintons as if they were friends.

Hillary has received letters from girls who wanted advice on careers. She has heard from working mothers having a hard time juggling the responsibilities of their jobs and their family. But she has heard from boys too. One wrote: "I think your position is very import[ant]. I want to be First Man when I grow up. I hope you do a good job."

Hillary was a little surprised to find so many people looking to her for answers. When she spoke to the graduating class at Wellesley, the First Lady had made it clear that she didn't think of herself as different from anyone else. "Most of us are doing the best we can to find whatever the right balance is for our lives.

"For me," she went on, "the elements of that balance are family, work, and service."

By setting high goals for herself and working hard to achieve them, Hillary Rodham Clinton has been able to make positive contributions in all three areas. She has raised a daughter, made a career in law, and served the public. Hillary has never been afraid to be a leader. At times this has made her unpopular, but she has also won respect, even from people who disagree with her. Hillary Rodham Clinton is an activist, someone who believes in strong action to achieve goals. By continuing to be an activist in the White House, she has changed the First Lady's role forever.

Highlights in the Life of
HILLARY RODHAM CLINTON

1947   On October 26, Hillary Diane Rodham is born.

1965   Hillary graduates from Maine South High School, Park Ridge, Illinois. She enters Wellesley College.

1969   Hillary becomes the first student commencement speaker in Wellesley's history. That fall, she begins studying law at Yale. She graduates in 1973.

1974   Hillary works in Washington, D. C., on the staff of the House Judiciary Committee. Later, she moves to Fayetteville, Arkansas, to teach law.

1975   On October 11, Hillary marries Bill Clinton.

1977   Hillary joins the Rose Law Firm.

1979   On January 10, Bill Clinton is sworn in as governor of Arkansas.

1980   Chelsea Clinton is born on February 27.

1983   As head of Arkansas's Commission on Education, Hillary pushes through statewide reform.

1993   Bill Clinton is sworn in as president of the United States. Hillary Rodham Clinton becomes first lady.

President Clinton announces that Hillary will lead a commission to study the nation's health-care system. Hugh Rodham, Hillary's father, dies. In September, President Clinton presents the health-care-reform proposal to Congress. Hillary Rodham Clinton appears before House and Senate committees. It is the first time a president's wife has testified on a major policy issue.

1994   The Senate Majority Leader announces in September that the Clinton Health Reform Proposal will not be pursued at this time.

For Further Study

More Books to Read

Facts and Fun about the Presidents. George Sullivan (Scholastic)

First Ladies. Rhoda Blumberg (Franklin Watts)

Hillary Rodham Clinton. Suzanne Levert (Millbrook Press)

Hillary Rodham Clinton, A New Kind of First Lady. JoAnn B. Guernsey (Lerner)

Videos

The Clinton Inaugural Commemorative. (MPI Home Video)

First Ladies. (Public Media)

First Ladies. (World Knapp Video)

107

Index